CHARACTERISTICS OF FACILITATORS:

THE ECUADOR PROJECT AND BEYOND

Arlen Etling

Center for International Education
School of Education
University of Massachusetts
Amherst, Massachusetts
1975

Copies are available from
Center for International Education
School of Education, Hills House South
University of Massachusetts
Amherst, Mass.

This book is dedicated to
Calvin S. Etling
one of the more effective
nonformal educators I have known

FORWARD

As the educational movement labelled nonformal education moves
beyond the initial stage of introduction and the fight for acceptance, a
consolidation phase begins. This book is an example of the more detailed
analysis which will characterize that second phase. The author has focussed
in on what is perhaps the most crucial element of nonformal education,
the facilitator or village level animator who is the central actor in determining
the success or failure of nonformal education. A better understanding of
what makes a successful facilitator and the subsidiary questions of selection
and training constitutes one of the prime research areas in the field of
nonformal education. This study makes a significant contribution to the
task of systematically describing and analyzing the characteristics of a
group of facilitators who have been working in rural Ecuadorian villages.

The author makes use of a modified Delphi technique to systematically
draw out the experiences of Ecuadorians and North Americans who have
been working to develop a feasible and effective approach to creating and
supporting village-level facilitators. Readers may be interested in studying
the method used by the author as well as the results. Methods of research
and evaluation which are appropriate for nonformal education are mostly in
the development stage. Further development of the Delphi approach may be
a promising avenue for the future. The reader will also find valuable the
lengthy section which reviews the community development and teacher

effectiveness literature. The author draws together research and thought from several widely separated fields and traces some of the parallel results as they relate to facilitators.

Finally, it should be noted that this study is the second book-length document to grow out of a project which is now in its fourth year of operation. The first study, written by James Hoxeng and entitled "Let Jorge Do It" forms a more general base upon which this work draws. As the author notes in his preface, the content and results are the products of a joint effort by a large group of Ecuadorians and members of the Center for International Education. All of the project staff joins the author in a common goal to make the results of our experiences available to all others who are struggling with similar problems and to encourage them to take from us whatever may be of help in their own situations.

David R. Evans
Amherst, Mass. 1975

TABLE OF CONTENTS

CHAPTERS

LIST OF TABLES

LIST OF FIGURES

SOME CHARACTERISTICS OF NONFORMAL EDUCATORS

Arlen Wayne Etling

ABSTRACT

The purpose of this study was to determine the characteristics of effective facilitators of nonformal education (NFE) in Ecuador in order to (a) more completely understand the nature of NFE; (b) evaluate the success of the Project; and (c) develop guidelines for training facilitators in other countries. Thirteen experts (six Ecuadorian and seven Northamerican staff members of the Project) brainstormed a list of skills, knowledge areas, and attitudes, of effective facilitators of NFE in community-based learning groups. The responses combined with items found in a review of literature of NFE, the Ecuador Project, community development, and teacher effectiveness, became the Preliminary List of Facilitator Characteristics. This list, consolidated into sixty general characteristics, was divided into (a) criteria for selecting facilitator trainees and (b) characteristics of facilitators after training. The sixty items became a second questionnaire. Each expert rated the appropriateness and importance of each item. The results of this second questionnaire were resubmitted to the experts to reconsider and rate a second time.

At least one-half of the experts agreed to the degree of importance of all except one item. Weighting the expert's responses resulted in a rank order of the relative importance of each item.

Two comparison groups with similar experience but little or no knowledge of the Ecuador Project also rated each item. The comparison groups confirmed the ratings of importance given by the experts. Variations between groups which occured in the rank order of items are apparently a result of experience with the Ecuador Project.

A process was also used to demonstrate how the general skills, knowledge areas, and attitudes, can be stated as observable behaviors for particular settings. Through this process, the operationalization of a goal or intent, the results of the study can be adapted to diverse settings and facilitator training programs can be elaborated for particular geographic and cultural situations.

The study also confirmed the utility of the Delphi technique in clarifying a group opinion. By providing feedback on the response to a previous questionnaire and by asking the respondents to reevaluate their individual opinions, a group consensus develops which research has shown to be more useful than an individual opinion, a single questionnaire, or a group discussion.

PREFACE

This study was inspired by my experience as a staff member for the
Ecuador Nonformal Education Project of the University of Massachusetts.*
Working in materials development and evaluation for the Project, I have
become increasingly aware of the "facilitator" idea being implemented in
Ecuadorian mountain villages. I believe that the facilitator idea is highly
transferable to different Bolivian settings with which I am familiar and that
the idea may be transferable to a large number of settings worldwide. I
also believe that the facilitator idea is one possible answer to the many crises
facing rural (and possibly urban) populations in developing countries.

But to adapt the facilitator idea to other settings depends on a fairly
complete understanding of how the idea works (and in some cases does not
work) in Ecuador. That information is not readily available. Much of the
information is in the form of observations and perceptions by Ecuador staff
members who have worked with the Ecuadorian facilitators. Therefore I
resolved to carry out this study in order to secure as much of that information

*The Ecuador Nonformal Education Project is a pilot program to
explore methodologies, techniques, and delivery systems, for nonformal
education in Andean Ecuador. The Center for International Education of the
University of Massachusetts and the Ministry of Education of Ecuador are
supported financially and administratively in this project by the U. S. Agency
for International Development.

xiii

as possible.

This study has not been sponsored by any organization or agency nor did I undertake the study at the request of any organization or agency. I did receive excellent cooperation from members of the Ecuador Project staff and I would not have been able to complete the study without their help, but during this study I was not employed by the Project. This study represents ideas, insights, and information from a variety of sources including Project staff but the study is not intended to represent the official position of the Project or any of its sponsoring agencies.

In addition to the members of the Ecuador Project staff, I would like to extend my sincere appreciation to David Evans, Sylvia Forman, Horace Reed, and George Urch. Each has made extensive and valuable contributions to this study. A note of thanks is also necessary to members of the Center for International Education for their comments and support, to Pauline Ashby for her advice and efficiency, and to my family for many and diverse contributions and sacrifices.

Arlen Etling

December 1974

University of Massachusetts

CHAPTER I

CRISIS IN THE CAMPO[1]

SOME IDEAS AND A MISSING LINK

This study is based on a series of primary assumptions: (a) there is

an educational crisis in the rural areas of most developing countries; (b) the

educational crisis is related to other crises such as food, population, energy,

economic development, political stability, social mobility, etc.; (c) the

school, as it currently exists, is unable to resolve the educational crisis;

(d) the ultimate solution to the educational crisis is an indigenous solution;

(e) local leaders are capable of providing education relevant to the needs of

their neighbors; and (f) it is desirable to identify and train such local

leaders then support them on their own terms as they develop educational

opportunities for their communities.

The Educational Crisis

Reimer (1970) maintains that

> Most of the children of the world are not in school.
> Most of those who enter drop out after a very few
> years. Most of those who succeed in school still
> become dropouts at a higher level. No child, however,
> fails to learn from school. Those who never get in
> learn that they do not deserve the good things of
> life. The later drop-outs learn that the system can
> be beat, but not by them (p. 1/1).

Coombs (1973) agrees and elaborates on the rural aspect of the educational

problems of developing countries:

> Despite two decades of valiant efforts to expand formal
> schooling, in the great bulk of rural areas (where the
> majority of people live) only a meagre fraction of boys
> and especially girls are getting a full and effective
> primary schooling. And of these, only a small
> minority have an opportunity to follow up their primary
> schooling in any systematic way. The unschooled and
> the early drop-outs--comprising the great majority--
> are left largely to fend for themselves (p. 1).

The failure of schools in meeting educational demands has been widely

documented. Both the school's internal weaknesses and its impact on

economic and social problems in developing countries have been discussed.

The Office of Education of the World Council of Churches (1970) estimates

that 30-40% of primary level pupils in developing countries drop out during

the first   two years. The school leaving exam is successfully completed by

15-25% of those who enter primary schools, but the majority are two to four

years older than normal age. Generally speaking the secondary school's

record is no better (p. 28).

Coombs (in press) feels that schools will be hardpressed to keep up

with population growth. Furthermore, "It would be unrealistic to suppose

that this situation will be dramatically altered in the foreseeable future

(p. 1/12)." McNamara (1973) agrees maintaining that 800 million people are

illiterate and, "despite the continuing expansion of education in the years

ahead, even more of their children are likely to be so (p. 7)."

The plight of adults is even more desperate since they are not normally served by the formal schools. In Ecuador, for instance, less than .5% of the education budget went to adult education (Plan quinquenal, 1972, p. 34). A survey of the allocation of public funds to adult education shows that many developing countries set aside less than 1% of the national budget for adults (World survey of education, 1971). If one source (The World Council of Churches) is accurate, training adults, especially in rural areas, must be a priority not only in order to increase national development but also to prevent the education of children from being wasted (Office of Education, 1970, p. 27).

Reimer (1970) maintains, "The conclusion is inescapable: no country in the world can afford the education its people demand in the form of schools (p. 1/2)." Even in the United States it is unlikely that schools can provide equal treatment, by educators' standards, for all students in primary and secondary schools. Illich (1970) estimates that such equal treatment by U. S. schools would cost eighty billion dollars annually (p. 12).

As a result of his research on schools Illich has called for the development of educational alternatives to schools. Other educators concur. In responding to the world's educational needs and the criticisms of school critics, many educators have turned to nonformal approaches as an alternative to formal education.

Nonformal Education

Historically nonformal education (NFE) includes activities which are

as old as mankind. As a term however, NFE represents an important change

in outlook "among both radical and liberal educators, concerned governments,

and social scientists (Bock & Papagiannis, 1973, p. 9). . . ." Since NFE is

such a new term there is a "lack of generally accepted terminology,

classifications, and basic assumptions (Coombs, 1973, p. 9)." It is

extremely difficult to define NFE satisfactorily.

> This is caused largely by (1) our present inadequate
> knowledge of educational activities carried on outside
> the formal school system, (2) the tendency of educators
> to think of education only in terms of formal, graded
> systems and (3) the wide-ranging and amorphous nature
> of nonformal educational activities, frequently private
> in origin and management and often achieved as a by-
> product of a venture primarily directed at objectives
> other than education (Brembeck, 1973, p. 138). . . .

Perhaps the most widely used definition of nonformal education is:

> . . . any organized educational activity outside the
> established formal system--whether operating
> separately or as an important feature of some
> broader activity--that is intended to serve some
> identifiable learning clienteles and learning
> objectives (Coombs, 1973, p. 11).

It is important to understand that NFE is not the antithesis of formal

education. Brembeck observes that NFE may substitute for formal

education for those who are denied schooling, "it may complement formal

education," or it may extend formal education maximizing its usefulness,

(Brembeck, 1973, p. xvi).

However, a definition of NFE and brief mention of the interface between nonformal and formal education is not sufficient. Some important theoretical dimensions of NFE must be set forth. Since NFE has many variations, each with its unique characteristics, the dimensions are not universal nor definitive. But some appear so frequently that they clearly deserve to be noted.

Kleis, Lang, Mietus, & Tiapula (1973) identify the following dimensions of NFE: it is (a) not likely to be identified as education; (b) usually concerned with immediate and practical missions; (c) potentially present at any learning site which affords appropriate experiences; (d) performance-based rather than by certificate-based; usually characterized by loosely organized content, staff, or structure; (f) characterized by voluntary participation; (g) usually a part-time activity of participants; (h) seldom graded or sequential; (i) usually less costly than formal education; (j) characterized by admission criteria which depend on the learner's need rather than on previously demonstrated ability; (k) served by educators who are chosen by demonstrated performance rather than by credentials; (l) not restricted to any particular organizational, curricular, or personnel classification, and it has great promise for renewing and expanding any of them; and (m) potentially conducive to multiplier effects, economy, and efficiency due to its openness, flexibility, and lack of concern for external and irrelevant criteria (pp. 6 & 7).

However, these dimensions do not describe all activities which fit Coombs'
definition of NFE. Some of the dimensions are inappropriate for some NFE
activities in certain settings.

Because NFE is characterized by diverse programs, projects, and
activities one conclusion is inevitable: the dimensions of NFE are situational--
they depend on the setting, the learners, learning objectives, resources,
sponsoring agencies, participating organizations, and unforseeable circumstances.

NFE Dimensions Important to Facilitator-Led Learning Groups

Since this study of characteristics of nonformal educators focuses on a
particular activity in Ecuador, facilitator-led learning groups, the author
will set forth his dimensions of NFE for that particular activity and setting.
These dimensions come from Kleis et al (1973), Paulston (1972), Evans &
Smith (1972), and the experience of the Ecuador NFE Project.

NFE should (a) be learner-centered as opposed to teacher-centered;
(b) feature a cafeteria curriculum of alternative learning opportunities;
(c) foster horizontal relationships among participants at every level; (d) rely
on local resources rather than imported resources; (e) be immediately
useful to learners; and (f) emphasize a low level of structure. These
dimensions will be more fully elaborated in Chapter II.

An Example of NFE

One of the promising approaches for NFE is the facilitator idea developed by the Ecuador Nonformal Education Project. In 1971 seven small villages in Andean Ecuador were invited to select representatives from among the residents to receive five weeks of training leading to the acquisition of skills, knowledge, and attitudes needed to facilitate learning in community-based learning groups (figure 1). The content of the training included communication and group process skills, critical thinking and problem solving, literacy and math skills, information concerning family life, and awareness of social, political, economic, and legal issues. Training emphasized the use of methodology and specially developed materials, related to the content areas. Upon completion of training, the trainees (facilitators) returned to form evening learning groups in their respective villages.

Ideally facilitators do not function as teachers but rather as organizers and coordinators of a variety of learning endeavors within the learning groups. Facilitators guide individuals in their learning groups in acquiring literacy, math skills, self-awareness, social awareness, ability to critically analyze local problems, and strategies for dealing with daily problems. A modified Freirean dialogue approach is employed by the facilitators in relating to the learning groups. On a more realistic level the facilitators' behavior is not always ideal.

8

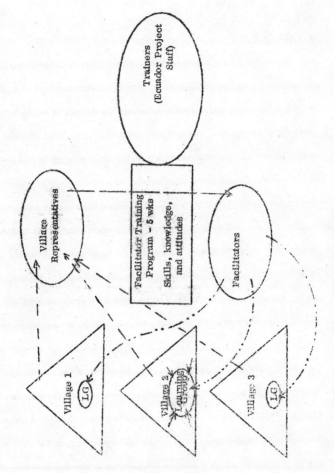

FIGURE 1: Facilitator Training in Ecuador

Subsequently training has taken place in a variety of settings. Responding to different conditions and building on previous experience, each training program has served as a step in an evolutionary process.

Swanson (1973) and Figueroa (1972) indicate that the facilitator model is successful to a degree and that the potential of the model in Ecuador is encouraging. However in spite of the success of the facilitator model in Ecuador, some weaknesses remain. There is no systematic preparation for the trainers. Facilitators are trained based on the experience and perception of a handful of trainers but there is little conceptual basis for the facilitator preparation. At least the conceptual base has not been identified and expressed. Apparently the trainers (Project staff) possess a variety of skills, attitudes, and knowledge which made it possible for them to design and administer a training program for facilitators. There is, however, no assurance that the same trainers could train facilitators for Mexican or Bolivian villages with similar success. Nor is there any assurance that a different group of trainers could duplicate the facilitator training in the same Ecuadorian setting.

If the potential of the facilitator idea is to be realized--if facilitators are to be prepared in other countries--and if the Ecuadorian trainers are not available to develop the training programs, other trainers must have guidance which will help them to train selected facilitators.

If facilitators are to be trained, however, there must be some clear understanding about how facilitators behave. Since facilitators are the important variable of community-based education in the Ecuador NFE Project, their behaviors are most critical. Nonformal education is a new field, however; therefore few projects in community-based nonformal education have been developed which focus on facilitator behaviors and attempt to conceptualize those behaviors. Information is lacking at this point.

The Problem

Research is needed to determine what skills, knowledge and attitudes are needed for effective facilitators of nonformal education in community-based learning groups. These skills, knowledge areas, and attitudes should be expressed as observable behaviors so that an observer from outside a learning group can determine if the facilitator is demonstrating desirable behaviors.

This research is needed if the facilitator idea is to be more fully understood and more easily transferable to new settings. At present the facilitator idea, a promising alternative which does not rely on expensive certified professional educators or costly facilities and materials, is largely in the minds of those individuals who have worked directly with facilitators.

Purpose

This study seeks to identify the important skills, knowledge areas, and attitudes, of effective facilitators of nonformal education in community-based learning groups. The opinion of a panel of experts will be sought in order to help identify and rate the importance of those characteristics of effective facilitators. The investigator also proposes to discover a way to translate general skills, knowledge, and attitudes, into observable behaviors relevant to particular settings. Those observable behaviors are necessary in order to evaluate the facilitator idea as it now exists and to train new facilitators for other settings.

Definitions

Facilitator: the uncertified, non-professional educator who develops and maintains village learning groups outside the formal schooling system.

To train: to guide, enable or facilitate learning of skills, knowledge, or attitudes.

To operationalize: to define a general skill, knowledge area, or attitude in terms of a list of observable behaviors.

Expert: present or former Ecuador Project staff member who has directly observed facilitators in Ecuador.

Significance of the Study

According to Coombs (1968),

> Intensified research is urgently needed to develop
> appropriate planning and evaluation techniques for
> nonformal education. All countries will be well
> advised to maintain a running inventory of such
> activities and to create mechanisms for assessing,
> planning, and harmonizing their far-flung nonformal
> education programmers (p. 177).

Coombs (1973) also feels that the first priority should be to "get equipped

as quickly as possible, by working together to develop the necessary

personnel, methods and new knowledge. . ." necessary to move ahead

rapidly in NFE (pp. 96-97).

Paulston (1973a) has called for research which examines attempted

innovations, identifies significant factors contributing to the failure or

success of the programs, and produces "credible evidence and theoretical

constructs which will enable us to explain, to predict, and to plan with

greater precision (p. 70)." This study of facilitator characteristics will

respond to Coombs' and Paulston's concerns for NFE research.

This study will also contribute to a fuller understanding of what is

meant by "NFE." Since no satisfactory definition of NFE exists, any

insight will be helpful. By identifying the skills, knowledge, and attitudes

of effective facilitators in a particular setting, more will be revealed about

NFE in that setting and, by extension, about NFE in general.

On a more practical level there is a resurging interest in rural educational development in the Third World. Organizations as diverse as the World Bank, The International Council for Educational Development, U.N.E.S.C.O., and the U. S. Agency for International Development (U.S.A.I.D.) have been advocating nonformal approaches to education in developing countries. U.S.A.I.D. recently awarded an institutional development grant to the Center for International Education at the University of Massachusetts (C.I.E.). The purpose of the grant is to develop the Center's capacity to consult where needed on problems of implementing nonformal education, especially problems pertaining to dissemination of information and training of educators. In order to develop that capacity to consult, more information on the characteristics of effective nonformal educators is needed.

This study is also significant to the Ecuador NFE Project. The Project's third year, April 1, 1974, to March 31, 1975, is designated a year of consolidation and evaluation. A list of skills, knowledge areas, and attitudes of effective facilitators would aid in that evaluation effort. By identifying the characteristics and operationalizing them to produce observable behaviors, the facilitator idea can be more objectively observed and evaluated. Newbry (1973), a U.S.A.I.D. official, concludes that the facilitator idea appears to work, though not in all cases. He wants to know much more about "characteristics of successful facilitators, conditions under which they can succeed, community acceptance (p. 9)." Evaluators on the Project staff have independently identified the same unanswered questions as important concerns. This study is directly relevant to those concerns.

The Ecuador Project staff are also interested in the transferability of the facilitator idea to other settings. Before the idea can be transfered, however, it must be more fully understood. Characteristics of effective Ecuadorian facilitators must be identified so that other groups can decide if the characteristics are relevant to a new setting. Once decisions are made as to the desirable characteristics for a new setting, then training programs can be designed.

Limitations

This is an exploratory study which will produce information needed to evaluate facilitators and to design training programs. The study does not attempt to develop an entire facilitator model; nor does it elaborate training programs for NFE. Rather, the study yields a list of facilitator characteristics which are important to more fully understand the facilitator idea as well as to guide the development of future training programs.

Many nonformal educators object to definitions, especially definitions of nonformal education at this point in its evolution. For the purpose of communication this study assumes Coombs' definition of NFE even though, by itself, the definition is unsatisfactory. A definition limits the spirit of diversity and flexibility of NFE.

Similarly, language is a limitation of the study. Most of the current educational terminology has come from the schooling tradition. Rather than propose a new vocabulary appropriate to NFE concepts, this study employs familiar terms. It is understood that such terms are used within the context established by the definition and dimensions of NFE specified earlier.

In regard to the Ecuador NFE Project the literature presents certain problems. Most of the information on the Project comes from unpublished documents. Some of those documents must be understood in view of the personality of the writer, the day-to-day pressures and concerns of Project staff, and the demands of forces external to Project activities. Some of the reports present a highly idealistic point of view. This limitation has been largely, but not completely, overcome by the investigator's experience as a member of the Project staff.

Research Model

The study is a descriptive and analytic view of the facilitator concept. It seeks to add conceptual strength to a part of the existing concept for preparing facilitators. Furthermore it identifies facilitator characteristics and confirms their importance through a panel of experts. In this sense the study is also a model-building study.

Increasingly literature is appearing which questions traditional experimental research models in educational research. Traditional experimental designs are prediction-oriented. The designs attempt to control certain variables which operate freely in learning environments. It can be argued, therefore, that the findings are not even generalizable to the real world conditions in which the experiment occurs. According to Stake (1969),

> As soon as we exercise a reasonable degree of experimental control, as soon as we provide some variability in the program and hold other aspects constant, the product is altered. Many an educator finds the program being researched no longer the program he wanted to know about (p. 41). . . .

Many educational evaluators are moving to more decision-oriented research. Evaluation activities in the Ecuador Project have definitely focused on data gathering for decision-making. As Paik (1973) observes "formative evaluation is essential but terminal summative efforts almost impossible (p. 184)."

Stake (1969) describes two approaches to educational research. "We have a fundamental choice: to be scientific, to generalize. . . to find out why; or to be descriptive, to be delimited. . . to find out what (p. 41)." This study chooses the latter alternative.

Assumptions

In attempting to describe, however, the investigator does not pretend to be completely objective. Certain assumptions are made which are a part of the study:

(a) What the facilitator is and does makes a difference in the learning in community-based nonformal learning groups.

(b) Whatever the facilitator does can be affected by training.

(c) Not all behaviors of effective facilitators, will be desirable for each facilitator.

(d) The facilitator will choose certain behaviors to practice but will not want to develop all of the desirable skills, knowledge, and attitudes of effective facilitators, at least not at once.

(e) Some of the facilitator skills, knowledge, and attitudes produced by this study may conflict with others making choices necessary.

Research Questions

The study will attempt to answer the following questions:

(a) What is the nature of nonformal education?

(b) How did the facilitator idea evolve in the Ecuador Project?

(c) What are the weaknesses of the Ecuador Project's facilitator model?

(d) What implications for an improved facilitator model can be gleaned from other literature?

(e) What general skills, attitudes, and knowledge do effective facilitators have?

(f) Can one develop a list of observable behaviors from these skills, knowledge areas, and attitudes?

Chapter II deals with the nature of nonformal education. The dimensions enumerated earlier in this chapter are discussed and other dimensions of NFE found in the literature are discussed. Finally some of the problems related to NFE activities are mentioned.

Chapter III traces the history of the Ecuador NFE Project, particularly in regard to the facilitator idea. Evaluation studies are analyzed and recommendations for improvements in the facilitator idea are presented. Suggestions for improvements are also solicited from literature on community development and teacher effectiveness. That literature is reviewed in Chapter IV.

Chapter V outlines the procedure for the study and discusses some ethical issues in social science research. The findings of the study are presented in Chapter VI and the last chapter summarizes and draws conclusions for the study.

Summary

The educational crisis in rural areas of the developing countries has been mentioned along with data which confirm the crisis. The inability of schools to meet this crisis has been cited and the potential of NFE in meeting the crisis has been briefly discussed. The Ecuador Project, an example of an NFE activity, has been introduced including the promising facilitator idea. If the facilitator idea of the Ecuador NFE Project is to realize its potential as an approach to resolving the educational crisis, however, more must be known about the characteristics of the facilitators. This study endeavors to discover and articulate those characteristics—the missing link.

CHAPTER I--FOOTNOTE

[1]"Campo" is a Spanish word which refers to rural areas. The word is used here for its poetic qualities, not because the rural educational crisis is limited to Spanish-speaking countries.

CHAPTER II

NFE--EMPOWERING THE POWERLESS

The title of this chapter reflects a value position. One of the most important functions, if not the most important function, of NFE is to empower the powerless--help them, individually and collectively, to become the principal determinant of their own lives. Only through learning to be subjects rather than objects can people begin to resolve the crisis in the campo.

The purpose of this chapter is to explore the nature of NFE in order to understand more about its strengths, its weaknesses, and its potential. NFE is examined as a concept and as a practical approach. Different NFE programs are mentioned to highlight the scope and diversity of the field. A conclusion is reached that the nature of NFE in local settings will vary. Therefore program developers should be aware of a wide range of possible NFE characteristics. The presentation of these characteristics in this chapter is divided into two parts: (a) those characteristics which are most important to facilitator-led learning groups (the focus of this study) and (b) other characteristics which are important to certain programs or writers but are not widely supported in the literature nor thought to be so critical to the focus of this study. Evidence supporting each of the characteristics is presented. Finally some of the general problems of NFE are discussed.

This chapter, then, should help clarify the nature of NFE so that the Ecuadorian facilitator idea can be strengthened conceptually and so that facilitators can be prepared in other cultural settings. Strengthening the facilitator idea and adapting it in other settings is one way to empower the powerless.

NFE as a Concept

Coombs (1973) sees nonformal education as a rather amorphous collection of diverse approaches, models, paradigms, and ideas, occupying a loosely-defined middle ground between informal and formal education. He defines informal education as "relatively unorganized and unsystematic (p. 11). . . " According to the same source formal education is

> the hierarchically structured, chronologically
> graded 'educational system,' running from
> primary school through the university and
> including, in addition to general academic studies,
> a variety of specialized programmes and institutions
> for full-time technical and professional training
> (p. 11).

Kleis et al. (1973) favor a continuum which includes incidental, informal, nonformal, and formal education. They define education as "the sum of all the experiences through which a person or a people come to know what they know (p. 3)." Incidental education is that enormously pervasive sector which includes "day-to-day direct and unexamined experiences of living" which shape the beliefs, habits, values, attitudes, speech patterns, etc., of people. These experiences are unintentional but powerful. When these same experiences are examined and deliberately augmented they constitute _informal_ education. The experiences may be augmented through explanation, interpretation, discipline, and example, by elders, employers, peers, and others. The augmentation may be intended as educative but the experiences themselves are not at least consciously, so intended (Kleis, et al., 1973, pp. 3-4).

What is more commonly called education is much more intentional and systematic involving deliberate selection and systematic structuring of experiences as well as the establishment of explicit missions, roles, and patterns of operation.

> To the extent that an education system is closely integrated structurally and substantively and tends to constrain each of its organizational, human and curricular components to its own stability or maintenance requirements it represents _formal_ education (Kleis et al., 1973, p. 5).

Kleis et al. (1973) see nonformal education as not closely integrated structurally or substantively. NFE tends to adapt to accommodate the requirements of missing or new components whether organizational, human, or curricular. They conclude that NFE is

> any intentional and systematic educational enterprise (usually outside of traditional schooling) in which content, media, time units, admission criteria, staff, facilities, and other system components are selected and/or adapted for particular students, populations, or situations in order to maximize attainment of the learning mission and minimize maintenance constraints of the system (p. 6).

Obviously there is overlap between formal and nonformal education which creates confusion. This confusion prevents an easy understanding of the conceptual differences between formal and nonformal education. Yet it is important that the conceptual distinction be made. NFE provides approaches to solving educational problems which the school has either created or has been unable to solve itself. The school's strengths and weaknesses must be understood so that clear options are made available to the educational planner. Otherwise nonformal educational activities may be co-opted and come to resemble the formal system. There is also the danger, which Dewey warned against, of selling old wine in new bottles.

NFE as a Practical Approach

On the other hand this conceptual distinction between NFE and formal education should not prevent their merger in educational pursuits. Harbison (1973) maintains, "The closer integration of nonformal and formal education may in the long run win the highest returns of all programs for human resource development (p. 10)." Once the relationship between outcomes and various inputs is understood "the issue is no longer the definition of nonformal education or even classifying projects according to some taxonomy. The issue is one of optimal design in specific settings (Evans & Smith, 1973, p. 16)." Coombs warns that formal and nonformal education should be seen as collaborative elements in a total system, not as antagonistic competitors (Coombs, 1973, p. 102).

The writer's position is that local conditions must determine the desirability and the extent of integration of NFE and formal education in each case under consideration. Such local conditions can best be assessed by the people most familiar with those conditions, the local learners themselves. In order to make decisions most beneficial to themselves the local learners need to become aware of the differences between NFE and formal education as well as the potential of each in a given situation. This awareness may come from within the learners, from external sources, or from both.

An external individual, organization, or agency which attempts to create awareness necessary for decision making must be very sensitive to those whose awareness is being raised. The external agent providing advice on NFE should also be aware of the characteristics of NFE which may be relevant to the local case. The agent will want to consider, in local terms, Coombs' practical question:

> What might be done through nonformal education . . .
> to help meet the minimum essential learning needs
> of millions of educationally deprived rural children
> and adolescents and to help accelerate social and
> economic development in rural areas (Coombs,
> 1973, p. 2)?

The "minimum essential learning needs" identified are (a) positive attitudes, (b) functional literacy and numeracy, (c) a scientific outlook and an elementary understanding of the processes of nature, (d) functional knowledge and skills for

raising a family and operating a household, (e) functional knowledge and skills

for earning a living, and (f) functional knowledge and skills for civic participation

(Coombs, 1973, pp. 14-15).

Although these learning needs appear to assume some of the author's

values (e.g. "Western" scientific values), a useful starting point is provided

by Coombs' list. Apparently, "No one mode or institution of education--formal,

informal, or nonformal--is capable by itself of meeting all of the minimum

essential learning needs (Coombs, 1973, p. 16)." Current programs require

redesign and reform, better integration, and supplementation by innovative new

programs. Rural development means transformation not only of production

methods and economic institutions but also of social and political infrastructures

and of human relationships and opportunities.

Another important practical question which NFE must answer is "education

for whom?" Again there is no pervasive answer. Most NFE proponents emphasize

groups neglected by the formal system. In New Paths to Learning for Rural

Children and Youth the neglected groups mentioned are young children, out-of-

schoolers, and girls (Coombs, 1973, p. 57). In The World Educational Crisis

adults are identified as a key group (Coombs, 1968, p. 142). Generally two

comments can be made concerning clienteles for nonformal educational programs:

(a) groups whose educational needs are not being met by schools are prime candidates; and (b) due to the huge number of people who have educational needs not being met by schools, priorities must be set and choices must be made. Too many times in the past educational priorities have been established which favor the priviledged. NFE raises the possibility of determining priorities which favor the powerless.

Varieties of NFE

Different NFE programs manifest different priorities, approaches, and characteristics. There is even considerable disagreement in NFE literature as to what constitutes an NFE program. This disagreement is apparent in various authors' attempts to provide broad categories into which NFE case studies can fit.

One typology divides NFE programs into the extension approach, the training approach, the cooperative self-help approach, and the integrated development approach (Swanson, 1973, p. 15). Another list of NFE program catagories includes adult education, continuing education, on-the-job training, accelerated training, farmer or worker training, and extension services. Sheffield & Diejomaoh (1972) in their survey of NFE in Africa, divide programs into the following categories: industrial and vocational pre-employment training; industrial and vocational on-the-job and skill-upgrading training; training programs for out-of-school youth in rural areas; training programs for adult populations in rural areas; and multi-purpose training programs. Another classification mentions indigenous learning systems, imported models, and recent homegrown innovations (Coombs, 1973, p. 41).

While all of these categories serve the authors' organizational purposes, none are satisfactory in practical terms. The categories force programs under more traditional labels which may obscure critical characteristics and profound differences among programs. No scheme has been presented that differentiates between NFE programs according to NFE characteristics which are important variables at the local level of decision making.

A start toward a more useful scheme was made by Coombs (1973) who highlights the differences between NFE needs in developing and industrialized nations. In the former emphasis is on useful skills and knowledge for national development, upgrading the competence of partially qualified people, serving school dropouts, and training rural leaders (p. 26). In the industrialized nations need for NFE focuses on pre-school children, on activities to parallel and complement formal schooling, and on follow-up for formal education (pp. 25-26).

Current examples of NFE mentioned by Coombs (1973) include pre-school day care, nurseries, school equivalency programs, adult literacy classes, boy and girl scouts, young farmers' clubs, sports and recreational groups, occupational training for adolescents in agriculture and construction carried on outside the formal school structure, centers for cultural improvement, work settlement camps, instructional programs in health, and apprenticeships. China is implementing a strategy of education as a part of rural development. Sri Lanka has a self-help community development movement inspired by Buddhist philosophy. Thailand has organized village newspaper reading centers. Colombia's Accion Cultural Popular uses its own radio network in conjunction with a weekly newspaper, low-cost textbooks, and supplemental readers (Coombs, 1973, p. 47-53).

Little can be learned about the nature of NFE from this list except that the examples represent diverse activities. Some of the activities on Coombs' list imply priorities, approaches, and characteristics which are associated with schools. The internal characteristics of those activities are not revealed.

In case studies Sheffield & Diejomaoh (1972) describe YWCA training programs for girls in East Africa. Botswana has developed work brigades to aid in development while training youth in construction, textiles, farming, handicrafts, leather tanning, and hotel keeping. Kenya's rural village polytechnics provide primary-school leavers with skill training applicable to local, rural self-employment. Agricultural settlement schemes for youth in Uganda provide gainful self-employment for school leavers, demonstrate the financial attractions of modern farming, and help revitalize a poor, under-populated area. At another level the Pan-African Institute for development in Cameroon trains for middle-level management positions in public and private development programs for seventeen African countries.

These African case studies provide more information about content, hence priorities. There is more emphasis on skills for self-employment and more attention to populations not served by schools. Still, the methodology, and objectives of the programs are not clear.

SENATI is a NFE subsystem created by Peruvian industrialists to train skilled labor. It is supported by a payroll tax and not only trains but helps employers assess their own needs and classify skills needed in their respective operations (Brembeck, 1973, p. 188). This program appears to be characteristic of schools. Based on the description given the priorities are not determined by the learners or even according to local needs. Educational goals and methods are determined by one group (employers) for another group (employees). Yet by Coombs definition this program may be considered an example of NFE.

Most of the programs mentioned fit Coombs' definition of NFE but the programs are so diverse that no clear perception of NFE emerges. Apparently Coombs' definition of NFE is not sufficient alone, as a criterion for NFE characteristics appropriate for particular local needs. Some elaboration of Coombs' definition is necessary. Also apparent is the diversity of activities labeled "NFE." If an NFE program is to be developed to meet the needs of a community-based learning group, more variables than Coombs includes in his

definition must be considered in order to specify appropriate characteristics
of NFE for the local setting.

NFE Dimensions Important to Facilitator-led Learning Groups

Six dimensions of NFE are emphasized in this study. These dimensions
are appropriate to local situations with which the author is familiar. A
discussion of these dimensions followed by discussion of other NFE dimensions
which are not emphasized will give a fuller understanding of the nature of
nonformal education.

Learner centered. Swanson (1973) states that in NFE participants create
a learning environment themselves rather than needing to have it imposed from
the outside (p. 15). Implied here is "substantial learner control over the
content and method (Evans & Smith, 1973, p. 14)." Therefore the learner must
participate in determining the objectives. A learner-centered environment
will help encourage more responsiveness of educational enterprises in adjusting
to changing needs or demands of learners, and hopefully, a more equitable
distribution of education opportunities will result.

Ward, Dettoni and McKinney (1973) call for educational goals that are
more practical and more closely related to the learners' needs (p. 112). A
pitfall to avoid is the adoption of imported models without tailoring them to local
conditions. Imported models may not be suitable for equipping learners with an
understanding of their physical, economic and cultural environment or with

knowledge and skills required for employment, household management, family

responsibility, and community participation (Coombs, 1973, p. 30 & 87).

According to one point of view the learner-centered nature of NFE

implies a performance-based learning model. Characteristics of NFE according

to Paulston (1972) include discrete content units and performance-standard needs

(pp. xii & xiv). "Emphasis is on acquisition of skills and the criterion for mastery

is competency which is often defined by the learner (Evans & Etling, 1974, pp.

3-4)." Brembeck (1973) claims that NFE should capitalize on trainees' individual

profiles of ability and motivation (p. 29). If these sources are correct then NFE

complements performance-based education since both place heavy emphasis on

individualization of learning.

Hilliard (1973) sees NFE as education, designed to pay its own way

through increased employment, productivity and social participation (p. 139).

Paulston (1972) echoes the focus on productivity and mentions job mobility as

another concern (pp. xii-xiv).

Whereas the schoolhouse tends to be the center of formal education, NFE

is more likely to occur at home or on the job. Part-time study and night study

are not unusual. Most NFE programs emphasize learning near the point of use

(Brembeck, 1973, p. 17; Paulston, 1972, p. xiii). All of these factors support

a learner-centered educational activity.

Most sources agree that self-awareness and power to control environment

are learner-centered attitudes which NFE strives to foster (Evans & Etling,

1974, p. 3). Attitudes are encouraged which lead learners to critically analyze themselves and their environment and to take positive action to resolve problems. Local initiative, self-help, and innovation are emphasized. Some scholars relate Paulo Freire's concientization[1] process to the goals of enhancing self-awareness, critical reflection, and positive action (Alschuler, pp. 1-2; Brembeck, 1972, p. 139). Freire's approach, however, is based on political activism which alienates some educators. The more enduring applications of Freire's ideas have been modifications which retain the learner-centered nature while softening the elements which tend to invite reaction and repression.

The mere emphasis on learner-centered education, however, may imply values which conflict with those reflected by the status quo and the elites (Paulston, 1972, p. xii). At this point NFE may not be able to avoid becoming politicized and controversial. It becomes vulnerable to powerful groups and individuals who see NFE as a threat to their positions. This condition may be disadvantageous; it may also be advantageous depending on the circumstances. At the other end of the spectrum NFE risks becoming a slogan for radical and revolutionary groups and individuals. The risk is that NFE may be seen as a general panacea which it certainly is not.

If the concern for learner-centered programs is of prime importance then the decisions will be made by the learners themselves in relation to their own practical problems. If NFE promoters limit themselves to meeting learners' expressed needs, there is less danger that NFE will become a target for

reaction or that it will be sold as an answer to all problems.

Cafeteria curriculum. Curricula in NFE tend to feature options, choices,

and flexibility rather than being sequential, prescribed, and required. This

tendency has led to the label "cafeteria curriculum (Evans & Etling, 1974, p. 3)."

Curricula are generated primarily by the learners and ideally,

> a strong effort should be made to discover the true
> interests, motivations, and wishes of the intended
> audience. The programme should then be shaped
> to fit these authentic concerns rather than the
> professional preconceptions and assumptions of
> outsiders. Even if it is discovered that the initial
> prime interests of the intended learners do not
> match what the programme architects might wish,
> they are still the most viable point of departure
> (Coombs, 1973, pp. 94-95).

A greater degree of local control is appropriate in NFE. Since distinct

groups must be identified due to scarce resources and specific skill and know-

ledge demands, decisions often must be made at the local program level

(Paulston, 1972, p. xii). Initiative, resources, enthusiasm, and human energy

must come in large measure from the rural people and communities themselves

(Coombs, 1973, pp. 78-79). NFE not only demands more local effort and

responsibility, it increases local capacity for responsibility and action.

Curriculum materials or delivery systems which might be considered

for NFE include radio programs (especially those of special interest to rural

people), rural educational features in newspapers, low-cost local news bulletins, market day exhibits, film demonstrations, posters, mobile libraries, and exchange visits (Coombs, 1973, p. 93). Various programs have used drama, role play, and puppets for motivation and for learning. NFE curricula should include participatory learning and entertainment using the vehicles of art as well as concepts of science and technology. All traditional nonformal education has a strong entertainment feature. Music, dance, plays, and epic narratives are often used (Brembeck, 1973, pp. 127 & 141). The resources and the skill for employing such curricula need not be imported nor developed professionally even for remote or economically poor villages.

Horizontal relationships. If NFE activities are to be learner-centered and individualized, if self-awareness and curricula generated by learners are to exist, then horizontal relationships, especially between learners and educators, should be emphasized. In this sense, the educators may want to view themselves in a different role: that of the helper, enabler, catalyst. A term used for this role is "facilitator." The facilitator is a paraprofessional or non-professional educator--perhaps one of the learners who has leadership abilities, more skill or knowledge at some point, or special training to serve as a facilitator in the community's learning group. Coombs (1973) calls for a strategy to capitalize on self-instruction and for teachers serving more as guides and coaches to learners rather than as drillmasters and substitutes for a textbook (p. 95).

In very poor countries, any rural education programme whose technology and effectiveness hinge on heavy inputs of fulltime professionally-trained instructional personnel at the local level, will in all probability be unable to expand sufficiently to serve more than a small fraction of the total potential clientele requiring such services (Coombs, in press, pp. 5/16-5/17).

In Attacking Rural Poverty, Coombs & Ahmed (1974) discuss the possibilities of using nonprofessionals:

The potential advantages of using local volunteers and other personnel (paid or unpaid) are several: (a) the impact of resources and personnel devoted to a program can be multiplied by using volunteers from the local community to assist in the educational effort as a model farmer, for example, or as a monitor of a radio listening group or an organizer of a youth or women's clubs; (b) a sense of involvement and participation in the educational program is generated in the local community by closely associating some of its members with the program; (c) the social and psychological acceptability of the educational messages is enhanced when the "opinion leaders" of the community are the educational agents for the program; (d) the use of local personnel can pave the way for changing the personnel structure in a program to allow a shift toward a smaller group of better paid and more qualified specialists and technicians in the field, while community people are enlisted for the simpler and less technical educational tasks (p. 217).

The nonprofessional facilitator, then, is in a much better position to support horizontal relationships among people than a professional teacher. Clearly horizontal relationships are important if NFE is to be learner centered and if learners are to choose from a cafeteria of learning opportunities. The role of the facilitator becomes that of helping a learner to choose and to interact with materials and master skills or develop knowledge and attitudes beneficial to the individual and the community.

Reliance on local resources. In developing countries NFE operates in conditions of economic scarcity. Therefore discovering inexpensive alternatives and relying on local resources is critical. Coombs (1973) warns against pilot projects which cannot be replicated on a large scale later or cannot be kept afloat long enough to test their time value. Likewise launching expensive longterm programs with only a few years of external support committed, or depending excessively on expatriate personnel, or constructing costly facilities with external funds which cannot be maintained with domestic funds, are all to be avoided. Educational planners are also warned against consuming substantial resources on an array of small and unconnected projects "that merely nibble at the edges of a huge problem (p. 87). . . ."

Since capital requirements for nonformal education are generally low, participants themselves may bear part of the costs (Paulston, 1972, p. xiii). Anderson (1973) observes that the cost of NFE can often be put to the account of the learner (p. 29). Such an arrangement encourages more responsibility and control on the part of the learner. More motivation is instilled in a program financed partially by the learner and greater program accountability can be expected. Hilliard (1973) suggests that NFE can pay its own way through increased employment, productivity, and social participation

(p. 139). NFE programs must rely on local resources as a matter of necessity. However by making reliance on local resources a matter of policy NFE provides a compelling alternative to the expense of schools.

Many nonformal programs do not require full-time facilities. A peculiar mentality often exists that views special facilities as a prerequisite for education. NFE, on the other hand, supports the assumption that education can occur anywhere. Use is made of facilities not intended for education so the costs of NFE are reduced. Often facilities and equipment can be rented or borrowed on a part-time basis. Sometimes participants themselves help build facilities. Also volunteers and part-time paid instructors are used as well as technical staff borrowed from government services and industry. The goals are to keep costs low without sacrificing quality, to get more resources from both conventional and unconventional sources, and to deploy available resources most efficiently (Coombs, 1973, pp. 66-69).

Immediate usefulness. NFE emphasizes "functional learning that bears an immediate and direct relationship to the life style of learners. A critical difference between formal and nonformal education is that NFE involves immediate action and the opportunity to put to use what is learned (Brembeck, 1973, p. 54). Payoffs therefore tend to be tangible and to increase material well-being (Paulston, 1972, p. xiii). Furthermore NFE activities tend to be short term with a present-time orientation (Paulston, 1972, p. xii). Nonformal education is superior to formal education "where the object is to change immediate action or to create new action (Brembeck, 1973, p. 54). . . ."

This dimension is particularly important as NFE attempts to meet needs related to the educational crisis in developing countries. Schooling solutions involve years, even decades, before the impact of a governmental decision manifests itself in economic benefits. By circumventing academic issues and bureaucratic pressures, however, NFE programs may be quickly implemented and the impact can be felt in a matter of weeks or months.

Low level of structure. As NFE programs are developed for different local situations, different approaches are required. Diversity of approach implies diversity, or at least flexibility, of structure. Paulston (1972) observes that many programs are uncoordinated, fragmented, and diffuse (p. xii). This condition may reflect a temporary, undesirable situation. However there is some advantage in diversity of NFE programs since, at this time, NFE approaches are still being developed conceptually as well as practically. Experimentation is encouraged which may lead to useful alternative structures. Another positive result of diversity is that local control of specific programs is easier than if NFE were completely within the supervision of a single national agency.

There is a great diversity in many aspects of NFE: the ages at which people are involved as learners, prerequisites, length of courses, and whether classrooms are used. Attendance is voluntary and varies. Likewise the amount

of documentation on enrollments, leaders' credentials, successes of those
involved in learning, increased economic well-being as a result of the courses,
and costs to the learners and the sponsors,varies greatly from one NFE program
to another (Brembeck, 1973, p. 17).

In contrast to schools NFE activities tend not to be age- or place-defined
(Paulston, 1972, p. xiv). Since voluntary participation is encouraged a greater
diversity of ages, sexes, and abilities can be found in nonformal programs. In
community-based learning groups this diversity is definitely appropriate.

Part of the low level of structure is exemplified in another NFE
characteristic, flexibility. There is flexibility in methods as well as timing
of activities (Paulston, 1972, pp. xii & xiv). NFE offers "more flexibility in
imparting skills and knowledge, more responsiveness in adjusting to changing
needs or demands, and hopefully, a more equitable distribution of educational
opportunities (Coombs, 1973, p. 63; Brembeck, 1973, p. xiv)." With its
flexibility NFE is more innovative and can more easily take account of sub-
cultures and minority needs (Evans & Etling, 1974, p. 4). Being less set into
fixed streams and curricula, nonformal training encourages flexible shifting
from one to another internal aspect as opportunities take on new patterns. A
typical case, due to the flexibility, is for an NFE program to strive to meet a
specific need and go out of existence when the need is filled (Brembeck, 1973,
pp. xiv & 29).

Due to the flexibility of NFE and its lack of affinity for national hierarchies, voluntary organizations are often involved (Paulston, 1972, p. xii). Such organizations, often headed by energetic amateurs who learn on the job, are frequently extraordinarily effective--more so than government programs managed by civil servants who often favor bureaucratic approaches. Another reason in favor of decentralization is expressed by Coombs & Ahmed (1974) who find that national plans "must be translated into more detailed development plans appropriate to each area (pp. 236-237)," therefore meeting the needs and conditions of each locality and population.

Summary. A review of the six NFE dimensions important to facilitator-led learning groups shows their interrelationship and interdependence. In a group led by a nonprofessional educator the learner will necessarily assume more importance choosing and pursuing educational activities. Horizontal relationships are necessary and desirable among peers who help each other rather than depending on an authority figure. In such a learning group where it is assumed that no single person knows what is "good for everyone else," alternative learning choices will replace sequential and standardized curricula. A local, autonomous, group which will not be able to depend on a hierarchical system for funds and resources will need to rely on local resources. As learners choose what to learn in economically limited conditions, they can be expected to prefer skills and knowledge which are tangible and immediately useful. Finally in considering all of the dimensions a low level of structure can be expected as learners make decisions and interact with each other in a situation where individual freedom, diverse priorities, and different individual needs and learning styles, are all present. These six dimensions are important to an NFE program which attempts to empower the powerless.

Although these NFE dimensions are appropriate for the NFE situation under study, they are not the only dimensions found in the literature. Other writers emphasize other dimensions or give a different interpretation for the six dimensions discussed above. Some of those dimensions will be discussed and reasons will be given for their not being considered as important for facilitator-led learning groups.

Other NFE Dimensions

Resocialization. Some NFE practitioners stress resocialization or de-colonization as an important dimension of NFE. Many proponents of this dimension are inspired by Freire's writings and experiments. Since so much attention has been given to this dimension it is worth examining Freire's position as summarized by Harmon. [2]

Freire is concerned with oppression which he defines as the lack of control over the significant decisions in one's life.

> There are three factors that have to be changed in an
> oppressive situation: the <u>Awareness</u> of the oppressed
> that they are oppressed and that they have alternatives;
> the awareness of the oppressor as oppressing; the system,
> which by its inequities rewards some, deprives others,
> dehumanizes all, yet as "system" is an abstract kind of
> concept; hard to attack, hard to change until its human
> components determine to become human (Harmon, p. 10).

Freire finds that the oppressor cannot make significant changes since he has too
much to lose. He also argues that no amount of benevolent assistance from
outside can make needed changes unless it actualizes the peoples' potential
and allows it to operate (Harmon, pp. 8-9).

Freire's approach is "political literacy," the ability to analyze the limiting
situation, the oppressor- oppressed relationship and in naming the situation, to
begin to transform it. His method has three components: initial awareness and
objectifying of the situation, reflection upon that reality with awareness of
alternatives, and action. "This reflection and action, leading in turn to further
reflection and action, he calls praxis." The actual steps of the Freire method
are: (a) an intensive hearing of the thought-language of the oppressed people in
their daily living condition; (b) an analysis of the thought-language, recorded in
some fashion by experts, followed by an evaluation of the analysis by the people;
(c) identification of the "generative words" of the people (those words which
contain central themes or concepts significant both in the culture and in the
political subjugation of the people; (d) encoding these words in pictures, slides,
or drama, which becomes the stimulus for discussion in groups called "culture

circles (Harmon, pp. 12-18)."

The goals of education for Freire is the development of "critical consciousness" in learners. To achieve this goal the leaders of the "culture circles" are admonished to remember their roles as facilitators of discovery, not as teachers who have the answers. Dialogue which expresses the consciousness of the teachers and students alike is the only allowable method. Together teacher-students and student-teachers are problem solvers (Harmon, pp. 15-19).

Dialogue, then, is the encounter between men, mediated by the world, in order to name the world (Freire, 1972, p. 76). The characteristics of dialogical action, for Freire, include: cooperation; unity for liberation, as opposed to division; organization as opposed to maniuplation; and cultural synthesis as opposed to cultural invasion (Harmon, pp, 22, 33-34).

This dimension of decolonization and resocialization holds as much danger as promise however.

> Freire's word will be co-opted. It will be taken
> into the classroom as a means of involving
> learners in their own domestication. His name
> will be used to legitimize new curricula, teaching
> techniques and technologies. He will become a
> guru among government planners, welfare workers
> and activists who are fighting to keep their jobs and
> their institutions alive (Williams, 1971, p. 81). . . .

There are indications that Williams' concern is not unfounded.

However this dimension is not included with the six dimensions preferred for this study for other reasons. Freire's ideas more than any other aspect of

NFE, have been relegated to the condition of a panacea. Freire is used as an excuse for making simplistic and artificial distinctions between individuals and groups (ones friends become the "oppressed" while ones enemies are the "oppressors" and people are labeled "oppressed" or "oppressors" purely on the basis of race or nationality). On a more fundamental level Freire's process of concientization involves professionals and implies an unequal relationship between the learners and the educators in some cases. So while elements of Freire's philosophy are included in the learner-centered dimension, other elements and interpretations of Freire are not appropriate for facilitator-led learning groups.

NFE complements formal education. For many sources this is an important dimension. Brembeck (1973) argues that NFE may maximize the benefits of formal education and he lists seven links between formal and nonformal education (pp. xv & 18).

If NFE is complementary to schooling, however, Hilliard (1973) argues that, "It is not third-rate formal education (p. 139)." Some advocates of NFE fear it will be viewed as a "wastebasket" into which those learners unsuccessful in schools will be thrown. If this is the case then NFE advocates might be diverted from developing valid, high quality educational activities for imparting skills and knowledge for "life."

This dimension is not emphasized for facilitator-led learning groups. The facilitator has no place in the formal school so it is awkward for him to complement a teacher. In many villages where NFE is needed, schools are not available. In other communities where schools are available the NFE program might be dominated or co-opted by the school since, as Illich has pointed out, the school is a powerful social institution which tends to encourage attitudes contrary to NFE.

A parallel system. Some authorities see in NFE a "parallel" educational system. Cuba's parallel system, China's spare-time prepartory middle school, and Peru's shadow school system are all mentioned as examples. However one source observes that difficulties may arise in local acceptance of such systems until the same degree of social prestige and rewards are attached to the parallel system as already exist in the formal system (Bock & Papagiannis, 1973, p. 16; Paulston, 1973a, 1973b). The author tends to agree with those sources.

Non-certificate orientation. Callaway (1973) states that NFE is not oriented toward diplomas, certificates and degrees (p. 17). Anderson (1973) maintains that "Preoccupation with certificates encourages officials to guide the economy in ways that can distort the prices of skills and thereby diminshes the amount of skill that can be employed (p. 29)." He also associates degrees, diplomas, and certificates with the emigration of skilled manpower and argues that NFE is less encouraging to such emigration. The author agrees with Anderson. However local learners in some cultures may demand certification of some kind. The important concern should be that certificates do not become an end in themselves. Removing certificates may only lead to their replacement by an equally artificial symbol. Furthermore, learners in NFE programs are not likely to use diplomas to emigrate. For these reasons this dimension is considered less important for facilitator settings.

Lifelong education. Coombs (1973) and Brembeck (1973) both see NFE, ideally, as a part of a "lifelong educational system." The need then is more diversification, better integration and much wider coverage of the whole population at all ages. Actually "lifelong education" as Coombs & Brembeck describe it implies some control and organization. Since this dimension is in conflict with learner-centered education and a low level of structure, the dimension is of doubtful significance. Although lifelong education is an important attitude for learners it is not considered a manageable feature of a particular NFE program. Lifelong education is not a likely feature of any "systematic" program. National governments have been generally unwilling, given present priorities, to consider funding education outside schools to a large degree. One interesting exception is Peru which is in the process of implementing a lifelong educational system.

Unsystematic. Both Harbison (1973) and Paik (1973) speak of NFE as "one of the most unsystematic of all systems." Callaway (1973) agrees observing that NFE activities are designed to accomplish many purposes. Therefore they do

48

not comprise a "system" but rather unrelated and uncoordinated "sub-systems."

Unfortunately some critics of NFE interpret this objective statement of degree

as a subjective statement of worth. So emphasizing this dimension would only

serve to undermine NFE.

Cost effectiveness. An important dimension for many educators is the

relative cost-effectiveness of NFE.

> Investment in particular types of out-of-school
> education may have more pronounced effects on
> economic productivity and social change in the
> short run (for example courses of learning while
> working) than is the case with formal schooling
> (Brembeck, 1973, p. 17). "

Other writers deal extensively with cost-effectiveness in evaluating programs

(Coombs & Ahmed, 1974, pp. 175-203; Coombs, 1973, pp. 68-70, 1968, pp.

17-97). However Bock and Papagiannis (1973) argue

> Unless one can demonstrate that both the cognitive and
> non-cognitive dimensions are similar in formal and
> non-formal educative activities in a comparative cost-
> benefit analysis, there can be no way to assess the
> substitutability of non-formal education (pp. 3-4). "

The author notes the criticism of Bock and Papagiannis in questioning this

dimension. Also questionable is the implication that accountants or economists

will determine which programs are acceptable. This decision should be left to

the learners.

Contributes to economic development. Another economic dimension which is commonly emphasized is that NFE should make a vigorous contribution to national development. Accordingly the priorities in developing countries for NFE must be work-oriented literacy and training programs which have an early impact on individual and national economic development (Brembeck, 1973, p. 185). Economic criteria, however, are not the only indicators of development. Human measures such as income redistribution, eradication of poverty, improvement of health-care systems, and more opportunity for meaningful civic and community participation, are considered to be as important as GNP for indicating development. So this dimension is strongly questioned not only because economic factors present an incomplete picture but also because it implies a national agency which sets priorities. The author feels priorities should be determined on a local level. Economic issues are important but economic decisions by outsiders are not highly desirable for a community learning group.

Indigenous education. Some persons feel that this dimension is the most important part of NFE. Proposed projects and activities are sometimes criticized because they do not resemble forms of indigenous education. Other activities are extolled due to their resemblance to indigenous education. On a more analytical level Billimoria (1973) finds useful insights and lessons in indigenous channels of education: the traditional concept of education in tribal life that stresses learning over teaching, the potential of indigenous infrastructures to transmit occupational skills, and the roles of a variety of professionals, para-professionals, and nonprofessionals as instructional agents of one sort or another (p. 33).

> The mother is in charge of the co-education of her
> children. In the evening she teaches both boys and
> girls the laws and customs, especially those governing
> the moral code and general rules of etiquette in the
> community. The teaching is carried on in the form
> of folklore and tribal legends. At the same time the
> children are given mental exercises through amusing
> riddles and puzzles which are told only in the evenings
> after meals, or while food is being cooked (Kenyatta,
> 1965, p. 100)."

As Nyerere (1967) points out, "The fact that pre-colonial Africa did not have 'schools'--except for short periods of initiation in some tribes--did not mean that the children were not educated (p. 2)."

Indigenous education overlaps heavily with what Coombs calls "informal" education. For this reason indigenous education is viewed as a source of inspiration, a repository of materials and approaches, and a clue to useful methods and techniques. Resemblance to indigenous education, in this study however, is not considered a dimension of NFE.

Other dimensions, which some sources included in their discussion of NFE, overlap with more-traditional subject-matter. Community development, rural animation, extension education, the cooperative movement, vocational education, and the behaviors of what some sources called "progressive teachers," are all possible dimensions of NFE which will be dealt with in the next chapter as independent points of view which may influence NFE.

Problems with NFE

Finally a discussion of NFE would be somewhat lacking if the more significant problems were not mentioned. NFE practitioners cannot make well-informed decisions concerning NFE if they are not aware of some of its weaknesses. For Illich the overriding problem is the monopoly of schools--their power to define education, appropriate most of the educational resources available, and brand any learning activities which take place outside schools as illegitimate (Illich, 1970). Coombs (1968) is concerned about the

> . . . lack of organizational means for bringing
> important forms of nonformal education within
> the purview of educational planning--since the
> latter has typically been confined to formal
> education and sometimes not even to all of that
> (p. 144).

Due to the monopoly of schools another problem exists: people who are running NFE programs may consciously imitate schools in order to gain respectability. Two gaps are noted in the methods employed by most NFE programs: the failure to make use of the large potential of radio and the general neglect of self-instructional materials to exploit the capacity of well-motivated people to learn from each other (Coombs, 1973, pp. 63-64).

Coombs & Ahmed (1974) see fragmentation of and between NFE programs as "one of the greatest handicaps not only to nonformal education but also to most other rural development efforts (p. 235)." Meager resources are too often wasted due to a lack of clear strategy, thorough planning, and workable

administrative arrangements of NFE programs. The whole field of NFE suffers

from fragmentation and overlapping of sponsorship and from the natural impulse

of each organization to pursue an independent course (Coombs, 1968, p. 144,

1973, p. 72). This independence of organizations and diffuseness of funding

sources leads to the proliferation of a large number of risky and costly pilot

programs.

Another limiting factor is that NFE is a largely unresearched sector of

education.

> In an analysis of 181 recent evaluation-research
> studies whose aims were behavior change, it was
> found that sixty-one per cent of the studies were
> school studies; only one per cent were conducted
> in non-formal educative settings (Bock &
> Pappagiannis, 1973, pp. 5-6).

Bock and Pappagiannis (1973) question the "paucity of social science

rigour" associated with implementation and evaluation of many NFE programs:

> without a more rigorous examination of the
> structural features of non-formal education and its
> social-psychological consequences on those who
> undergo its processing, we might continue to create,
> fund or encourage educative activities that do not
> include variables related to the ultimate objectives
> of development education (pp. 5-6).

There is also some question as to whether NFE contributes to equitable

rural and local development. NFE may change the occupational structure without

providing any more relative social advantage (Bock & Pappagiannis, 1973, p. 5).

It may benefit those who are already better off and seriously neglect the most disadvantaged, thereby widening the socio-economic gaps within rural areas (Coombs & Ahmed, 1974, p. 237).

At another level NFE is susceptible to political factors which can make or break any policy.

> Nonformal education programmes are heirs to particularly difficult political problems. Their natural constituency is fragmented and much of it has a weak political voice. The subjects they deal with cut a wide swath across the specialized interests and jurisdictions of numerous official bureaucracies and private organizations (Coombs, 1973, p. 75).

The nature of the Freirean rhetoric, as this chapter has shown earlier, also makes its promoters particularly vulnerable to political opposition, reaction, and repression.

Finally NFE may be regarded by many as a panacea or as another world-wide fad. NFE is certainly not a perfect solution to all educational problems. However NFE does hold much more promise than fads which often degenerate into superficiality and result in eventual disillusionment. If NFE is not to be seen as a panacea then its true nature--its strengths and weaknesses--must be understood.

Summary

This chapter has analyzed the nature of NFE--its strengths, its weaknesses, and its potential. Since the study is concerned with the characteristics of non-

formal facilitators in community learning groups, NFE has been analyzed from
that particular perspective. Six dimensions of NFE which seem to have particular
relevance to that perspective have been discussed. Those dimensions are
(a) learner centered; (b) cafeteria curriculum; (c) horizontal relationships
(d) reliance on local resources; (e) immediate usefulness; and (f) low level of
structure. Other possible dimensions of NFE, which have a lesser degree of
relevance to the study as well as less general support in the literature, have also
been presented. Finally a number of problems, which have been associated with
NFE, have been discussed in order to provide a fuller understanding of nonformal education.

Conclusion

Throughout this chapter there is a temptation to view NFE from one of two
antagonistic points of view: NFE as a means of strengthening the educational
establishment of a nation; or NFE as a means of subverting that establishment.
Some individuals see the dilemma in terms of a contradiction: NFE as an
approach for government planners to develop and integrate into the educational
system; or NFE as an approach for community leaders in meeting the educational
crisis caused by the national educational system. The writer suggests that these
may be false dichotomies, at least in many cases, and that advocacy of one of
the viewpoints in opposition to the other viewpoint may be a trap which can lead
to endless bickering and energy-draining rivalry. The dilemma can be resolved,

as the title suggests, by an emphasis on "empowering the powerless" in a primarily educational sense. National educational agencies can, and have, set out to meet the immediate individual needs of those people who have been traditionally neglected by schools. Furthermore national development goals need not contradict local individual or community needs. The key, however, is sensitivity to the individual and community levels of education. Although uncommon in practice it is possible for national educational policies to serve the people, especially the traditionally disenfranchised. Where governments or school systems openly discriminate, where they are a means for insuring social inequality, NFE may only be productive to the extent that it subverts that educational establishment. However to be preferred, when possible, is a more constructive attitude of empowering the powerless as a means of national, community, and individual enrichment. Empowering the powerless may be a means of uplifting all members of a society without overthrowing any of those members. That is the challenge of NFE.

CHAPTER II FOOTNOTES

[1]Briefly concientization refers to a process of becoming conscious of oneself and one's environment, developing a conscience--a feeling of personal responsibility--for social and psychological contradictions in oneself and one's environment, and taking action to resolve those contradictions. The process is more fully discussed later in the chapter.

[2]Freire's two principal books, Pedagogy of the Oppressed and Education for Critical Consciousness, are difficult reading. Following Frieire's argument is not always easy. On the other hand Harmon provides a summarized and well organized discussion of Freire's philosophy which is faithful to the original sources. For this reason Harmon is the principal source of citations of Freire's thought.

CHAPTER III

THE ECUADOR NFE PROJECT--HOW JORGE DOES IT

One project which has attempted to develop strategies for resolving the crisis in the campo through nonformal educational approaches is the Ecuador NFE Project. This Project is the center of attention of this study for three reasons: (a) the author's experience as a member of the Project staff inspired the study; (b) the facilitator idea which is the focus of this study grew out of the Project; and (c) it is the one substantial NFE activity most accessible to the author.

The purpose of this chapter is to present a brief history of the first two years of the Ecuador Project in order to clarify the development of the facilitator idea. Next evaluation efforts related to the Project will be reviewed to help determine the strengths and weaknesses of the facilitator idea. Finally recommendations of three principal evaluators will be summarized. This look at the Ecuador NFE Project's facilitator idea will provide the basis for a list of characteristics of effective facilitators. The list of characteristics, in turn, will be a useful conceptual tool to guide the improvement of the facilitator idea in Ecuador and to help prepare facilitators for other cultural settings.

Results of minor evaluation efforts which confirm certain particular aspects of the Project will be reported in the discussion of those aspects. Three major evaluation efforts, however, will be discussed in a separate section at the end of the chapter.

Due to the purpose of the chapter a large number of Project activities will be mentioned only superficially in order to concentrate on the facilitator idea--the way Jorge does it. Jorge is a metaphor of an effective Ecuadorian facilitator as perceived by the Project staff.[1] He is also a real facilitator in Ecuador who has already had one book, Let Jorge Do It (Hoxeng, 1973), named after him.

Origin and Objectives

The Ecuador NFE Project traces its origin to the spring of 1971. After preliminary discussions between the Center for International Education of the University of Massachusetts (C.I.E.) and U.S.A.I.D. officials working in Ecuador, a feasibility study team was formed. The team, consisting of representatives of C.I.E., U.S.A.I.D. and a private Ecuadorian educational organization visited thirty different government and private programs, institutions, and projects in Ecuador which were engaged in non-school educational activities.

> The goals of the study were to identify on-going projects,
> to assess the potential of existing institutions to make
> use of nonschool education techniques, and to assess
> the willingness of these institutions to try out new
> procedures (Evans and Hoxeng, 1972, p. 1).

As a result of the study team's efforts and discussions among U.S.A.I.D., C.I.E. and the government of Ecuador, a new image of education in Ecuador emerged. This image featured low-cost universal basic education where control of the learning would be retained by the learners themselves. Prerequisites would be eliminated and traditional classroom teachers would be replaced by non-professional educators. With this general image in mind a contract was signed by C. I. E., U. S. A. I. D., and the Ecuadorian Ministry of Education (M. O. E.) to begin on April 1, 1972. The objectives for the project as outlined in the agreement are:

1. Create and field test a range of non-formal educational techniques using local institutions to implement and support these techniques in field situations.

2. Develop a number of non-formal educational methodologies which are feasible for use by existing Ecuadorian institutions.

3. Implement selected methodologies with institutions, including the Ministry of Education, with on-going evaluation system designed to provide both current as well as terminal evidence of program impact.

4. Make methodologies available to other interested agencies and provide support for their efforts.

5. Devise and test training procedures to carry out these methodologies and use of support materials.

6. Provide technical assistance in non-formal education to the Ministry of Education. Assist the Government of Ecuador and other Ecuadorian institutions to develop non-formal education projects (Swanson, 1973, pp. 2-3).

To implement this contract a Project staff was formed.

Split between Quito and Amherst the Project staff is organized for mobility and flexibility. In Amherst the staff consists of the principal investigator, secretary, administrator, materials development specialist, and evaluation specialist, of whom the last three are graduate students. In Quito all except the field administrator are Ecuadorians, a change in standard U.S.A.I.D. policy. A project director, field coordinator, evaluation specialist and materials development specialist, are aided by secretaries and associates. Some additional staff members have been hired for short-term, product-oriented activities (Evans & Etling, 1974, pp. 4-5). From this staff the Project's organizing ideas developed.

Organizing Ideas

Project staff believe that all cultures, are rich in potential educative devices which are unexploited for educational purposes; that a vast array of non-traditional educational carriers exist and can be adapted across cultures; and that "penny technologies"--the lowest denominator of local or foreign technology--have potential as carriers of educational messages and ideas. So a project hypothesis developed:

> that the level of effectiveness of campesino community members would be increased to the extent that they would better utilize the already existing processes of non-formal education, and take advantage of the action promoted by the facilitators being trained under the program.

They defined these terms as follows:

> Effectiveness: The individual's inclination and
> capacity to influence and transform his own
> environment.
>
> Non-formal education: The information and
> instruction that one receives apart from the
> formal school system such as primarys, high
> schools, universities, and traditional literacy
> centers.
>
> Facilitators: people from the community itself,
> trained by the program, who are not teachers in
> the traditional sense but serve as resources that
> promote, catalyze and stimulate learning through
> using the non-formal education processes (Ickis,
> 1973, p. 3; Newbry & Applegate, 1973, p. 1).

Soon after beginning the first contract year in April 1972, the Project's philosophy began to emerge. Because anticipated materials and delivery systems followed no existing pattern, because of the difficulty in conducting a sophisticated research effort initially, and due to the backgrounds and personalities of Project staff, a strong action orientation has developed. Host country leadership has been emphasized from the beginning along with a decision to keep North American presence in Ecuador to a minimum. Non-specialization has become a watchword. The Project intention has been that tasks are shared and everyone is kept informed of the activities of the others. Eschewing a standardized curriculum the "different strokes for different folks" theme has emerged. The idea of a cafeteria of learning opportunities has allowed rural Ecuadorians to select what appeals to them. Another curricular decision was to stress functional learning--knowledge and skills directly useful in daily living.

Non-professional manpower has been an organizing idea based on the beliefs that education does not necessarily require someone labeled "teacher" and that requiring all educators to be professionals is an unnecessary extravagance for developing countries' governments. Materials have been developed which are inexpensive, easily reproducible, motivating, immediately relevant, and self-explanatory. Materials have been seen as part of a self-generating curriculum of unfinished and adaptable products and opportunities. Since a decision was made not to build a centralized bureaucratic model of NFE, complementarity of distribution systems (concentrating on different segments of the population or going about education for different reasons and in different ways) has been a basic criterion. To help promote complementarity of distribution systems a policy of free access to information, especially in relation to educational organizations and agencies, has been followed. Finally the Project has sought to stimulate community-based decision and demand systems,

> in which people become aware of themselves as
> resources and begin to develop "survival skills"
> required to interact with agencies: (1) the
> ability and willingness to approach the appropriate
> source of information or material; and (2) techniques
> to get a reasonable hearing from organizational
> representatives, politicians, and educators
> (Hoxeng, 1973, p. 27).

In order to implement these ideas a number of non-formal approaches have been considered. The most intriguing of these is the facilitator idea. But the facilitator idea did not only grow out of an innovative educational attitude on the part of Project staff. As much as any factor the facilitator idea grew out of the conditions and attitudes of the Ecuadorian campesino (peasant).

The Facilitator Idea

After an analysis of those conditions and attitudes the following change objectives were established:

- Increase campesino's self-confidence;
- Obtain more active participation by women in community decisions;
- Develop the desire and ability to take advantage of existing resources without waiting for everything to come from other strata, chance or destiny;
- Increase campesinos' aspirations;
- Encourage development of community and personal planning, oriented to taking action and solving all kinds of problems; and
- Increase community collaboration, between community members and with facilitators.

Promote -community participation;
        -greater participation in family and community decision making;
        -use of dialog by the campesino as a basic element in all the informal processes.

Increase the number of functional literates, people that not only can read and write but can use information and at times question it.

Promote - reading of newspapers and magazines and listening to radio;
- possession of newspapers and magazines in homes.

Promote - concern for obtaining more information about topics that interest them and for knowing where to get the information;
- better sanitary habits;
- greater concern for a better diet.

Work toward - less paternalism;
- reinforcement of internal leadership;
- greater shared leadership (Ickis, 1972, pp. 4 & 5).

An idea, consistent with the Project's educational philosophy as well as the change objectives, was elaborated. Selected communities which agreed to cooperate would select two or three residents to become facilitators of non-formal education. These community representatives would receive training from Project staff members. After training the new facilitators would return to their villages to work toward meeting the change objectives proposed by the Project staff, (see Fig. 1, p. 8).

Six rural Mestizo communities which reacted favorably to the facilitator idea, after a brief introduction of the idea by Project staff, were selected for the first facilitator project. Criteria used in the selection of the communities were:

1. Mestizo rather than Indian.

2. Accessible by road.

3. Little previous development agency intervention.

4. Similarity to other selected communities, in terms of:
    a. income
    b. agriculture as primary occupation
    c. Population from 500 to 3000 people
    d. resource base sufficient for potential economic viability

5. Openness toward the project and to possibility of change.

6. Illiteracy rate sufficiently high to be viewed by the community as a problem (Hoxeng, 1973, p. 72).

All six communities were located in the Andes, near each other.

Criteria recommended to the communities for the selection of facilitator trainees were:

1. Have completed third grade (later amended to the behavioral criterion of being able to read and write).

2. Be living with their families (parents or spouse).

3. Be active in community affairs.

4. Be able to work at least two months full-time on the project.

5. Be dynamic and open.

6. Have lived in the community for at least a year.

7. Have demonstrated interest in community development.

8. Have personal growth aspirations (Ickis, 1972, p. 10).

Some communities which were selected used those criteria while others did not. Some of the facilitator trainees were nominated and elected democratically, some were selected by community leaders, and others were self-selected.

The First Facilitator Training

The first facilitator training, in October, 1971, was conducted by C.E.M.A.[2] trainers. Twenty-four campesinos from the six communities participated. They met ten hours each day. Group dynamics exercises designed to reduce tension filled most of the first week's schedule. The second week focused on exercises which introduced the community development approach. Hacienda, a board simulation game was introduced leading to discussion which stressed critical analysis of oneself and the socio-political environment. Participants established their own learning objectives for the training at this time. During the third week games and materials for literacy and numeracy learning were introduced and discussed. After a week in their respective communities applying and considering what they had learned in training, the facilitators returned for the fifth and sixth weeks of training. During those final weeks participants developed plans for activities which they would carry out in their communities.

A newly adapted literacy method, which had been developed by the trainers, was introduced. This method, inspired by the philosophy of Paulo Freire and calling on the experiences of a number of educators, is based on the literacy method of Sylvia Ashton-Warner as described in her book, Teacher (1963). The trainees practiced this method among rural populations as a part of the training.

The training was heavily process oriented including skills in working with groups, ability to communicate, and problem solving and critical analysis skills. Achievement motivation activities emphasized establishment of goals, planning strategies for elaborating goals, overcoming obstacles, taking risks, and using outside assistance. Information was also provided concerning health, hygiene, nutrition, how to reach information sources, how to use the information, how to discriminate between critical and unimportant information, and how to take advantage of the existing political and legal system (Hoxeng, 1973, pp. 66-68; Ickis, 1972, pp. 11-18).

According to Patricio Barriga, the Project field director and a trainer,

> Training was very ambitious because this was our first attempt as trainers to create facilitators. We were still developing in our minds what "facilitator" meant, and consequently, what training they should receive. There were disagreements among the trainers, mostly behind the scenes. Perhaps the training was too long. It might have been better to have a shorter initial training and more intensive followup training sessions spread over a period of six months. The major problem was to convince the prospective facilitators that they were capable of teaching others. We never really did

> achieve this goal until much later in their communities
> when their own experience proved to them, some of
> them, that they were able to "facilitate" learning in
> their friends and neighbors (E. P. D. , 2).[3]

Some of the results of the facilitator training were immediately obvious,

however. A government official who had been attending the sessions

commented at the end of the sixth week:

> But how these students have changed! It's impressive!
> They have more confidence and a greater sense of
> personal pride in their work. Now they talk and discuss
> among themselves and they even walk differently--
> with their heads held high (E. P. D., 12).

The new facilitators returned to their respective villages and began to

organize NFE activities. Evening learning groups were organized in the six

villages involving about 150 learners. Most of the groups met five nights

each week for the duration of the eleven-month agreement negotiated with the

facilitators. Work was begun on twenty-six community development projects

of which thirteen were completed, two failed and eleven were still being

pursued as of March, 1973, eighteen months after the facilitator training

(Hoxeng, 1973, p. 66). Projects included installation of running water and

electricity, building schools, repairing community buildings, making road

improvements, a bridge renovation, a community draining project, organizing

a concrete block factory, forestation, and organization of cooperatives.

One of the more interesting outcomes of the facilitator training was

that within eighteen months some of the facilitators had not only carried out activities in their own communities but had planned, organized, and conducted three ten-day training sessions for 45 representatives of 12 new communities (Hoxeng, 1973, p. 67). The first, and most completely documented of these facilitator-run courses was at Tutupala.

Second Generation Facilitators

Four active facilitators, aided by Project staff in the planning stages, negotiated with C. E. M. A. for training funds. The objectives for the training were:

1. That the campesinos from the participating communities place a higher value on their own self-worth.

2. That campesinos teach each other to read, write and negotiate (Hoxeng, 1973, p. 110).

After laying the groundwork in the new communities the facilitators negotiated with regional officials for approval, participation, food, housing, and materials. A budget was developed and accepted and the facilitator course was planned.

Beginning on November 20, 1972, the course proceeded according to a carefully elaborated plan:

Monday--welcome; creation of confidence among the participants; determination of seminar schedule with the participants.

Tuesday--discussion of the nature of the seminar; sharing of problems in the community--general dicussion; who-am-I exercise; Hacienda game.

Wednesday--discussion of Hacienda game; blindness experience; discussion of problems in communication.

Thursday--discussion of specific problems and interests of each community.

Friday-- discussion of how campesinos are treated by authorities.

Monday--demonstration of the six steps of the modified Ashton-Warner literacy method; practice of the steps.

Tuesday--sociodrama on the teaching of literacy; discussion.

Wednesday--practice of the modified literacy method in community groups; reflections on the method; Hacienda game again.

Thursday--blind leap experience; discussion of problems in applying the literacy method; introduction of other fluency and simulation games; making personal copies of letter and number dice.

Friday--negotiation of plans for each community; review; farewell (Hoxeng, 1973, pp. 116-117).

One of the Project staff members who had helped the Tutupala facilitators plan the training observed, "The performance of the Tutupala facilitators was impressive. They were at all times in command of the situation without dictating what went on (Hoxeng, 1973, p. 118). . . ."

Staff reports indicate that without a doubt campesinos can work effectively as trainers of their peers, that communication is easy, that participants are responsive, and that the trainers effectively use the techniques and methods that they learned previously (E.P.D., 14, p. 9). That the campesino trainers had sufficient confidence in the techniques and methods, in them-selves as trainers, and in the receptivity of the trainees, is a strong indication of the feasibility of the facilitator-run training approach.

Other Facilitator Training Courses

Active facilitators, Project staff, and C.E.M.A. trainers collaborated to organize and conduct other courses for preparing facilitators. Three different groups were trained in these courses: members of predominately Quechua-speaking communities; members of coastal communities; and women.

Training Quechua facilitators. In order to test the generalizability of the facilitator approach to Quechua speaking communities, a course was presented by two of the Project staff in the Parrish of Columbe during June, 1973. The course objectives were similar to those of the previous facilitator training programs. Communicating mainly in Quechua representatives from nine communities participated in the training. During the mornings of the first week dialogue sessions attacked several themes basic to rural develop-ment in Ecuador: "we want to prove to ourselves and others that we are capable of doing something; who am I; at what times in our lives did we cease to be humans; why are we poor; why do we conform (E.P.D., 1)?" During the afternoons, activities were organized to create group unity and confidence. Other activities included in the three weeks of training were discussion of participants' plans for work in their communities, film-viewing and discussion, practicing the use of games and other educational materials, developing competence in the modified literacy method, and discussion of survival skills for life in rural Ecuador.

Although only one trainee expressed any interest in community development or educational work at the beginning of the training, all but two of the participants organized activities in their communities after the course. Observers report improvement in communication not only in the facilitator groups organized in each community but also within and between communities represented at the course. Characteristics of new critical awareness were also noted as they were employed in community activity for self-improvement. Finally there is evidence of increased knowledge, not only in fluency and numeracy but also related to survival skills, community organization, and negotiation with outside organizations and agencies (E.P.D., 1, pp. 35 & 44).

Training for women. Another course, in March of 1973, prepared nineteen women from seven communities in group dynamics, dialogue, educational gaming and the literacy method. Although there was little follow-up, reports indicate that the course led to a variety of activities in the improvement of the participants' communities (Hoxeng, 1973, pp. 121-125).

Training on the coast. In October, 1973, participants from seven coastal villages participated in yet another facilitator training course. Venturing into a completely new area (geographically and culturally) than they

had worked with before, Project staff presented a more streamlined course.
In an intensive three-day program the same topics were raised as with
previous facilitator training groups. Group dynamics exercises, discussion
of problems and experiences in the communities, introduction of educational
games and materials, and development of a plan of activities for each
participating community, were included in the course. Materials were
produced or disseminated for use in each community (E. P. D. , 1).

A Closer Look at Jorge

An understanding of the facilitator idea is incomplete however without
a closer look at the individuals who participated in the facilitator training.
Swanson (1973) describes a composite of the facilitator:

> He is approximately twenty-five years old and works
> on a small two or three hectare farm in the mountains
> of Chimborazo or Tungurahua. He earns approximately
> sixteen to twenty dollars a month growing potatoes,
> beans, corn, or barley, and selling them in the local
> markets. He grows small agricultural products also
> for home consumption. Married, with one or two
> children, he lives with his family in a small adobe
> shack. There is no electricity nor water in his home,
> but he is proud of his home and tries to make improve-
> ments. He is basically optimistic about bettering
> himself, although he has no illusions of becoming rich.
> His dream is to obtain more land, earn more money,
> better his present home, and give his children a better
> life. Although he began primary school, he dropped out
> after two years of education to work the farm with his
> father. School was not particularly an enjoyable place
> for him, but he did learn to read and write sufficiently
> to help others in his present facilitator classes. He is
> skeptical about what the government can do to help the

rural population in Ecuador, and since joining the
facilitator program he realizes even more the
ultimate responsibility rests on his own efforts.
Attitude and behavioral changes are coming fast
these days, as the program is changing him to
become a new man. Profound changes are taking
place in his views of life, what he wants to do with
his life, and how he can accomplish new things
(pp. 44-45).

It is also essential, in grasping the facilitator idea, to understand the

interaction between the facilitator and his peers in the learning group:

Just after dusk, campesinos begin to leave their mud-
walled houses and walk toward the school. They have
no light; their feet know every bump of their half-hour
walk. By 7:30 about twenty-five people are collected
around the dark concrete-floored building. One of the
campesinos arrives with a petromax lantern and a key.
They all enter, and after suitable pumping and preparation
the room is reasonably well lighted. There is still a
constant problem of shadows, as the lamp cannot be
hung high enough for the light to shine down from above.
Three of the campesinos take charge; until this time
they were undistinguishable from the rest of the group.
Two circles are formed; the participants use the school's
desks or sit on the floor. One group will choose a game
from the three or four which the facilitators have brought.
The other will use the Ashton-Warner adaptation ("el
metodo de Sylvia"), writing in notebooks and on the board.
People choose their group. The game proceeds with much
more interpersonal assistance than competition-conscious
Americans would be comfortable with. Each player is
surrounded by at least two fellow participants acting as
coaches. Play is intense, but is punctuated by outbursts
of laughter. The Ashton-Warner group concentrates on
writing in notebooks, aided by two of the facilitators who
circulate quietly among the intent students.

After two hours, the groups come together to talk
over some of the ideas which have emerged from the
Ashton-Warner group. This night the discussion
centers around the possibility of obtaining running
water for the community. The facilitators guide the
conversation without dominating it. They ask question
after question. Participants aged twelve through fifty
contribute their ideas, receiving positive reinforcement
from the facilitators. No conclusion is reached; there
will be time for that in coming sessions. As the
session ends, one of the participants makes an announce-
ment in his capacity as chairman of the town council
and leads a short discussion. About ten o'clock the
lantern is extinguished. Small groups move off in a
dozen directions, wrapping their ponchos more tightly
against a cold misty rain. They leave quickly; the
work day begins about 5:00 a.m. (Hoxeng, 1973, pp.
65-66).

Project Conclusions

After two years of Project involvement in training local facilitators it

is possible to draw some conclusions. The concept itself has several

advantages:

1. It puts education in the hands of the people themselves;
2. it reduces the cost of education;
3. it increases the potential of a horizontal and,
   consequently liberating educational relationship,
   without the vertical and often domesticating
   student-teacher relationship provided by formal
   schooling; and
4. it provides open and flexible access to educational
   opportunities without the need for a fixed curriculum
   and institutional requirements (E. P. D. , 17, p. 11).

In a book-length case study of the Ecuador NFE Project, James Hoxeng,

the first field administrator of the Project concludes:

76

1. A felt need for literacy is sufficient motivating force to bring a portion of the people in a campesino community together for daily meetings for a period of several months.
2. Campesinos without extensive training can conduct classes for their peers, and are acceptable to them as "facilitators" who eschew traditional trappings of leadership.
3. Rural populations have little difficulty entering into dialog and reflection on topics that arise from their literacy exercises.
4. The combination of literacy and dialog facilitates movement of these groups toward development planning and to action on concrete projects.

5. Not only the facilitators but also other participants in the classes can change their behavior vis-a-vis authority figures, becoming more efficacious in their dealings.
6. The above process is aided by games to reinforce learning, to conceptualize relationships, and to break down stereotypical images of the learning situation.
7. Further, the above mentioned facilitators can design and run training courses for campesinos from other communities, thus creating new cadres of facilitators.
8. The dialog concept can be extended to radio schools through the use of cassette tape recorders as a feedback device, allowing participants freedom to decide what they wish to do with the recorder. This seems to have some effect on self-image.
9. Organizations and individuals involved in development education are open to new ideas and techniques, and will pick up on them for use in their own programs without external incentives (Hoxeng, 1973, p. 190).

That facilitators use the materials and dialogue method much as they are trained to do has also been concluded. Therefore "training is a major factor of how facilitators conduct their sessions." Furthermore, "The only discernible learning goal evident is teaching what participants appear to be interested in (Swanson, 1973, pp. 47-48)." This conclusion verifies one of the Project staff's assumptions about learner-centered education.

In regard to skills, knowledge, and attitudes, "The facilitator role seems to consist of a mixture of community development agent, discussion leader, counselor, with some of the behaviors of teachers--particularly teachers who work in open classrooms (Evans & Etling, 1974, p. 31)." Smith, Tasiguano & Moreno group the skills, knowledge, and attitudes of facilitators into six broad areas: life experience, self-image, ambition, attitude toward authority, and attitude toward problem solving (E.P.D., 20).

There are some interesting questions however, which the Project has not yet answered. Hoxeng (1973) concludes that more needs to be known about:

1. Whether the facilitator phenomenon works only in the small areas where we've tried it.
2. How long the model will continue to function, or what form it may take in later stages.
3. Whether the model will in fact prove to be self-renewing.
4. If the games are an integral part of the short-run success of the project, or if they represent only a peripheral gringo-sponsored activity.
5. Whether the organization and staff of the project is a crucial factor--i.e., whether the materials and ideas can be implemented effectively by others (pp. 191-192).

So far these questions have not been answered conclusively. However a review of evaluation reports on the Project gives some hints to the answers of those questions. Other questions and concerns are also resolved by the evaluators.

Evaluation Efforts

Probably very few pilot programs in rural education in a developing country have been evaluated so intensely as the Ecuador NFE Project. A number of evaluators have focused on a wide range of Project activities, techniques, assumptions, and impact. Some of the efforts are very comprehensive; others are quite specific. Most evaluation has been done by Project staff, however several outside evaluators have been employed by U.S.A.I.D. Conflicting evaluation reports tend to confirm that the individual evaluator's perspective is the most important variable in evaluation of the Project.

One outside evaluator hired by U.S.A.I.D. states,

> this project could become a landmark in the re-
> conceptualization of education for the entire world.
> The landmark could easily be of the magnitude of
> significance of the Chinese educational reform and
> the original land grant philosophy in the mid-
> nineteenth century (E.P.D., 21, p. 1).

After this extremely optimistic introduction the evaluator raises issues and draws conclusions which demonstrate his lack of understanding of the Project as well as an insensitivity to the organizing ideas of the Project, the possible effects of outside intervention in the facilitator communities, and the previous evaluation efforts made by the Project staff. This particular evaluator had been unable to visit Project personnel prior to his visit to

Ecuador. Once in Ecuador he was unable to visit any of the communities where facilitators were working. The conclusions reached by him, although they were advanced only in the context of an evaluation proposal, must be discounted.

Staff evaluation. Project staff have been under continuous pressure from the beginning by U. S. A. I. D. to evaluate various aspects of the Project. An evaluation specialist is included in the Amherst staff as well as the Quito staff of the Project. Case studies as well as analysis of cost and relative effectiveness of various games have been compiled by the staff. Much of the Quito evaluator's work has been concerned with pilot testing of materials before they are introduced in the villages. Baseline data on rural Ecuador has been accumulated through the use of an interview questionnaire in a study unrelated to the Project. Project staff, however, have repeated the questionnaire twice at yearly intervals and have added a section to the questionnaire which enables evaluation of the introduction of radio programs with campesino-oriented content. Also nine technical notes on general and specific aspects of the Project have been written by the staff. Although very helpful in guiding decision-making, these efforts have not satisfied U. S. A. I. D. 's desire for "hard data" on specific questions.

In an attempt to respond concretely to a question about the learning outcomes of educational games created by Project staff a laboratory experiment was carried out. Project evaluators conclude that "relatively brief exposure to the Multiplication Bingo game can significantly increase numeracy skills

but only when there is a good deal of psychological investment in the game."

Also,

> Apparently thirty minutes of playing the Letter
> Rummy game can improve scores on our test
> by about forty per cent. However, approximately
> half of this gain comes from increased familiarity
> with the test (E. P. D., 9).

Since this test was not replicated, due to considerable cost in time and

expense, the results are not conclusive.

In addition to evaluating specific aspects of the Project, the staff have

also assessed the overall organization and activities. Hoxeng (1973) found

that certain values, which are held by Project staff, pervade the Project.

Some of those values are

> that school provides very little possibility of
> reward to rural dwellers, but that other more
> utilitarian educational alternatives exist; that
> acquisition and improvement of property is a
> necessary factor in bringing about any change in
> the present situation; that working together is
> virtually essential; that information is a valuable
> source of power (1973, p. 1). . . .

Another value judgement involves the teacher-student relationship in

educational activities. Implicit in the facilitator role as developed in Project

training is the notion that everyone is a student at one time or another; that

the student is responsible for his education; and that the role of the educator

is to catalyze and to encourage learning but never to attempt to give another person knowledge. Project staff have also taken a position on literacy, namely that literacy may not be the greatest educational need of the rural poor. Furthermore if literacy is a goal then the purposes for learning must be determined by illiterates. Learning to read and write (a common goal of literacy programs) may not be congruent with rural Ecuadorians' goals and opportunities. Therefore Project personnel have not been disturbed when learners dropped out of a literacy program after learning to sign their names.

On a more critical note, Gillette, in a review of a film by and about the Ecuador NFE project points out a number of value positions held by Project personnel which he considers questionable:

> First, that it is in fact possible to win within the existing conditions and power relationships. Second, that the cause of the peasant's precarious economic situation lies within himself (implicitly since in the past he has not bought land and invested in fertilizer). Third, that peasants have (or can obtain at reasonable rates) sufficient capital to buy enough land and invest in enough fertilizer to make a significant difference in their living standard (Gillette, 1973, p. 136).

Again more questions than answers come forth. For more conclusive results more comprehensive evaluations must be consulted.

Major evaluation efforts. Three efforts by non-staff evaluators provide considerable insight into Project strengths and weaknesses especially in relation to the facilitator idea. Swanson's study was commissioned by

U.S.A.I.D. officials in Quito. It is carefully elaborated and comprehensive

in nature. A C.E.M.A. evaluation (Figueroa, 1972) provides a needed

Ecuadorian perspective to the evaluation attempts. Like Swanson's study

the C.E.M.A. effort is comprehensive and sensitive to the particular nature

of the Project and the villages. Finally a shorter and more focused evaluation

by Forman (E.P.D., 6) looks critically at the facilitator idea in three

villages. Forman's findings fill gaps in the other two studies since her

perspective is that of an anthropologist who speaks Quechua and lived in one

of the villages for several months.

Project Strengths

Swanson finds several advantages in NFE as it has been implemented

by the Project:

1. Non-formal students receive instruction that is more
   relevant to their immediate needs than found in formal
   education programs. Fostered by relevant educational
   materials, non-formal learners receive instruction
   in accordance with needs of daily life.
2. Methodology exposed to students is more likely to lead
   to changing attitudes and behaviors than methodologies
   implemented by formal adult education.
3. Participants learn survival skills that help them
   participate more in the community and discover how
   to change their situation. Participants compile
   "survival skill catalogs" that contain materials,
   information, procedures, and approaches for handling
   community problems. These skills that participants
   compile, after discussion, help them face Ecuadorian
   reality.

4. Literacy learning is coupled with technical skill learning which has applicability to the rural sector. By emphasizing a multi-pronged approach of literacy training, consciousness raising, skill enhancement, and self-awareness techniques, it avoids the real spector of a lack of learning environment in rural areas. Participants create a learning environment themselves--in the rural sector--rather than needing to have it imposed from outside (Swanson, 1973, pp. 14-15).

He also concludes that NFE stimulates adults to read and write as effectively, or more effectively, than formal adult education programs (Swanson, p. 22). Furthermore Swanson (1973) observes that NFE classes benefit learners through attitudes embedded in action situations:

Attitudes formed in classes have particular functional significance for the participant--the goals he pursues, the values he hopes to maximize, and the coping process in which he is engaged (p. 105).

Swanson (1973) is favorably impressed with the games developed by the Project. He asserts that the games have made an important and positive contribution to innovative education in Ecuador and elsewhere and that they meet the needs of the learners (pp. 23 & 35).

With regard to facilitators Swanson (1973) states that they are excellent in attending classes regularly and that they teach games and the dialogue method much like they are trained. Training, according to this evaluator, is a major factor in how facilitators conduct their sessions (pp. 45-48).

Summarizing the benefits of the Project Swanson (1973) cites:

1. Development of thirty games that will be used by the
    facilitator centers throughout their existence.
2. Involvement in attitude change and action change that
    have created some thirty-odd community development
    projects, with expectance that with the new facilitator
    centers an additional twenty to thirty other community
    development projects will be started.
3. Enhancement of functional skills that will enable
    participants to receive new agricultural information,
    information about health and nutrition, and skills to
    help themselves (pp. 108-109).

In the C.E.M.A. evaluation Figueroa (1972) mentions community

development in the area of the greatest Project impact. Though the original

Project orientation was toward literacy and numeracy as a means to

community development,

> it still left room to take a different orientation, which
> is what actually happened, being dialogue and reflection
> the parts of literacy which turned out to be of greater
> use for the "campesinos." This is for me the value of
> this Project, where the expected results were produced
> by means which turned more to the "campesinos" own
> needs (pp. 10-12).

Furthermore the Project has had a greater impact in those communities

where the facilitator has had an attitude of participation and change. A

participatory learning style certainly contributes to another C.E.M.A.

finding: that strengthening of leadership within communities is an important

contribution of the Project.

Finally Figueroa (1972) applauds the manner of intervention in the

communities of the Project. "If compared with other experimental projects such as U.N.E.S.C.O.'s Pilot Literacy Project, the cost of this Project is less (p. 13)." Moreover the facilitator has been able to maintain interest once it has been aroused in the community; a quality, "which is very rare in other literacy centers (p. 13)." Lastly, this evaluation concludes, "there has not been an 'imposition of values' which other projects can rarely claim (p. 13)."

Summarizing the strengths of the Project which have become apparent in the first two years of the experiment, one must include the use of non-professional change agents (the facilitators) who have been capable of initiating community-based education and development activities as well as training peers to function in the same role. Training time and costs have been low. Materials developed have been used consistently, interest has been maintained from the time of introduction, and the cost of implementation has been low. At least ten organizations have used at least fourteen Project techniques in activities which have directly involved 1700 people in their use. Observable learning has taken place as people have used Project materials both for periods of a few minutes and over a number of months. Some of the techniques and the dialogue method have appeared to be directly correlated with community development activity (Hoxeng, 1973, pp. 105-107, 188-189).

Project Weaknesses

The C. E. M. A. evaluation's greatest criticism of the Project is the lack of followup by Project staff after the facilitators have been trained. Swanson, Forman, and Hoxeng also note this shortcoming. Followup responsibility has been accepted by the Project but it has not been fully accomplished and "some of the facilitators complain of not having received enough support (Figueroa, 1972, pp. 8-11)." Forman observes that facilitators do not have regular contact with Project staff members. She also uncovers another aspect of the problem: "The facilitators who trained together do not form a 'support group' for each other (E. P. D. , 6). . . ."

Swanson (1972) is concerned with a lack of understanding of the Project by the villagers--their ignorance of Project objectives and opportunities. He criticizes the "methodology without a system" citing that participants have little notion of where the dialogue method will lead (Swanson, 1972, pp. 20 & 24).

Swanson (1973), like many observers from outside the Project, is struck by the unsystematic approach which the Project takes in certain areas. He notes the lack of a systematic delivery system for introducing Project materials and methodologies to formal institutions and other interested agencies. He criticizes the Project for lack of sequence in developing games and for not systematically introducing all games in all of the facilitator communities (pp. 25 & 34-35). In all fairness one must observe that sequence is a concept more appropriate to a relatively fixed curriculum and that the Project has consciously chosen and maintained a policy of free choice of materials and methodologies on the part of facilitators, learners, and cooperating institutions. To have been more systematic Project staff would have been required to be more authoritarian and aggressive--approaches which conflict with the Project's organizing ideas. Another evaluator, however, supports Swanson, at least in a general sense, maintaining that the Project is "too non-directive (E. P. D. , 6, p. 17)."

Swanson (1973) also notes the scarcity of material provided to facilitators and suggests the Project could have been more thorough in this regard. He also feels that some facilitators lack sufficient training in the use of games and methodology. Another gap in facilitator training is the question of how learners move from being completely illiterate to begin the process of becoming functionally literate. "The process spelled out in Teacher and in Project documents does not explain this point (pp. 33-34 & 42)." Figueroa (1972) suggests that the purpose and relevance of literacy to the campesinos should be examined. She observes that the learning of writing and math seem to have been of little use for the campesinos in community development (p. 14).

"Facilitators and participants expressed a concern for legitimizing their activities, and would readily accept certificates that would demonstrate that validity of operation (Swanson, 1973, p. 26)." Project staff have consciously avoided certificates which were thought to be associated with formal education. It seems, however, that the prestige offered by community-based education in the facilitator groups is an issue.

The drop-out problem is another of Swanson's concerns. He maintains that students stop attending or tend ". . . to be confused with time limits involved in the learning process (Swanson, 1973, p. 24)." Again there seems to be a problem of evaluating the facilitator groups by standards and assumptions held by advocates of schooling. Swanson, himself, notes that the drop-out rate in the facilitator groups compares favorably with drop-out rates for government adult education centers. However, Hoxeng (1973) explains that drop-outs are replaced and that no stigma is attached to irregular attendance.

> The facilitator project was consciously organized on a non-schooling model, however, so people felt free to attend long enough to learn to write their names, for example, and then to leave--perhaps for good, or perhaps to return another day with other needs (p. 94).

Another criticism of Swanson's (1973) which is also controversial, is his contention that no apparent national organizations or institutions were brought into planning and initiating the Project (p. 18). The criticism is misleading since thirty Ecuadorian organizations were contacted during the feasibility study. Furthermore, the Project staff, including almost as many Ecuadorians as Northamericans, decided to develop and try the unconventional ideas which emerged from planning before involving organizations more accustomed to traditional approaches and bureaucratic modes of operation. However Swanson's implied fear, that the Project might end without having developed the national institutional basis for the ideas to continue, is genuine. Hoxeng (1973) is also concerned with the facilitators' relationship with the outside support agency. He, unlike Swanson, is as concerned with the paternalism of Ecuadorian organizations as he is with the lack of Ecuadorian institutional support (p. 103).

Forman's report on the facilitator groups in the villages of Colta and Columbe mentions the persistence of the "traditional formal educational format in the literacy classes (E. P. D. , 6, pp. 12-13)." She suggests that part of the problem might be due to a lack of sufficient "de-schooling" during the facilitator training. As a result of a facilitator behavior which is often close to the teacher role, the decision-making behavior of the learners is limited.

A conceptual problem with the facilitator idea is also revealed by Forman:

We (meaning the Amherst and Quito staff, especially
the Northamericans) have a strong inclination to view
a person's social roles as very distinct or separated
from each other. People who spend their lives in
small, relatively closed communities, conversely,
tend to view others as "totalities," in which all the
social roles an individual has are interlinked and
inseparable. Hence, when a new social role (e.g.,
facilitator) is introduced, it must be integrated into
the total role set of the individual and into the set
of role-expectations of the community, if difficulties
are to be avoided (E.P.D., 6, p. 15).

Recommendations

All three evaluators make recommendations based on their respective

studies. Since there is considerable overlap the recommendations have

been consolidated.

In regard to general conceptual issues the evaluators recommend:

(a) that the facilitator idea should be employed in communities which lack

schools and adult education projects; (b) that the established community

leadership and a large portion of the residents be informed of the facilitator

idea and of their potential association with it before the idea is implemented;

(c) that overall Project organization be examined; (d) that other delivery

systems (radio, rural mimeo newspaper, programmed instruction) be

explored; (e) that research and evaluation activities be expanded; and (f) that

the literacy process be more completely conceptualized.

The evaluators are unanimous in recommending some screening of possible trainees before they are accepted as facilitators. Figueroa (1972) suggest that "status" should be used as a selection criterion.

Concerning facilitator training, (a) the trainees should be thoroughly prepared in all materials and methodologies to be used; (b) intensive "deschooling" followed by resocialization of facilitators is crucial; and (c) the trainees should be encouraged to develop detailed and specific limited goals as well as general large-scale ones, which they wish to pursue in their communities after training.

With regard to facilitator intervention in the communities the following recommendations are made: (a) employ facilitator "teams" to avoid individual isolation; (b) integrate the facilitator role into the set of role expectations of the community; (c) create roles related to the facilitator for established community leaders; (d) focus materials and methodologies more on families; and (e) encourage more effort by facilitators to secure community support for their activities.

Once facilitators are working in the communities the Project staff are admonished to (a) provide for more communication between facilitator communities; (b) provide more supplies as well as other economic and logistical support; (c) carry out a very strict coordination and follow-up plan for facilitators to include in-service training, formal support groups, motivation, introduction of new materials, and support of a non-formal "network communication system"; and (d) encourage facilitators to provide more alternatives during learning sessions.

Recommendations were also made concerning the Project staff's relations with groups outside the facilitator villages. The Project should provide more training for educational institutions outside the Project including rural cooperatives, formal schools, social and community organizations, etc. On the other hand strict controls were encouraged of people and institutions which are allowed access to Project operations.

It should be remembered that evaluation of the Ecuador Nonformal Education Project is incomplete since the Project is still active. Already Project staff members are attempting to respond during the third year to many of the issues raised above. The third year according to the Project contract is to see a major effort in evaluation and consolidation.

Conclusion

This historical overview and the evaluation reports give a clearer indication of how the facilitator concept developed as a part of the Ecuador NFE Project. The evaluations indicate where changes can be made to improve the facilitator idea. From this discussion a clearer understanding of Jorge-- an effective facilitator--his role in the village, his skills, knowledge, and attitudes, and his potential, emerges.

But the full potential of the facilitator idea may not be realized if the conceptual base is limited to nonformal educational literature and the experience of the Ecuador NFE Project. Other sources and approaches relevant to the facilitator model must be examined to provide new insight into an improved facilitator concept. The examination of those sources and approaches is the subject of the next chapter.

CHAPTER III--FOOTNOTES

[1]A metaphor is appropriate in this chapter to represent the wide diversity
of personalities, abilities and backgrounds, which are found among facilitators.
The introduction of a metaphorical element is also appropriate to this
Project description for another reason. Much of the documentation of the
Ecuador Project is available only through unpublished letters, memos,
reports, and field notes of Project staff. There is a tendency for those
sources to emphasize a slightly more idealistic viewpoint of events than
an outside observer might accept. The author has attempted to deal
conscientiously with this issue in order to present a sensitive and accurate
description of the Project.

[2]An Ecuadorian consulting group started under U.S.A.I.D. financing and
specializing in achievement motivation, organizational activities, and
educational programs.

[3]Unpublished Ecuador Project documents (E.P.D.) are included on a special
reference list after the bibliographies. Each reference is numbered so
(E.P.D., 2) is number 2 on the list of Project references.

CHAPTER IV

THE COMMUNITY AS A CLASSROOM

THE CLASSROOM AS A COMMUNITY

So far the facilitator idea has been examined in terms of NFE literature and the Ecuador NFE Project. This chapter deals with literature from more traditional fields which are also relevant to the facilitator approach. Literature reviewed here is divided into two broad areas: community development and teacher effectiveness.

As the title suggests the review of literature in each of the two areas is conducted from a particular perspective. Community development literature is approached in terms of its contribution in aiding the facilitator to use the community as a classroom. Beyond the role as a coordinator of an evening learning group the facilitator must relate to the community at large in order to be effective. Community development approaches, as reflected by conceptual writings and case studies, are useful to the facilitator who is interested in providing individuals with community-based learning opportunities as well as encouraging community development through individuals' educational activities. Concerns more particular to community development (e.g., the relative merits of community development approaches) are not the focus of this chapter.

The literature reviewed here dealing with teacher effectiveness, likewise, does not cover every aspect of that subject. Much of the literature on teacher effectiveness deals with issues and behaviors which are more relevant to a traditional teacher role. However some of the teacher effectiveness sources treat the teacher more as a facilitator than as an authority figure. Those sources have much to contribute to an improved facilitator concept. In order to distinguish between the two teacher roles a criterion is used: which sources view the classroom as a community where shared decision making, horizontal relationships, learner responsibility, and flexibility predominate? The sources which fulfill that criterion generally are relevant to the facilitator idea.

The purpose of this chapter, then, is to survey the literature dealing with community development and teacher effectiveness as it contributes to an improved facilitator concept. Furthermore the more helpful sources are briefly explained so that the reader may return to them for a deeper understanding of some particular discussion that may be more relevant to a certain NFE setting than it is to the focus of this study.

Community Development

A review of the literature on community development leaves one strong impression: most community development writers assume an outside intervention, usually by professional staff, as the focus of development activity in the local community. The possibility of a self-perpetuating, completely indigenous model is not mentioned. Furthermore like NFE community development activities are quite diverse. A large number of isolated experiments provide variety which may be useful but handicap communication and understanding. There is also confusion and contradiction resulting from different conceptions of the development process.

Coombs (1973) observes that the general literature on development is not very helpful in answering three questions: the role of rural areas in national development; the criteria and evidence appropriate to judge progress of rural development; and the manner in which the process of rural development gets started and unfolds (p. 20). Part of the reason for this observation is that much of the literature on development tends to be quite general and theoretical focusing on national needs. In order to answer Coombs attention must be focused on the human element and the perspective must include that of development from the local level upward as well as the perspective from the national level downward.

Starting with Batten, one of the foremost authorities on community development around the world, this section examines the role of community development and a general definition. Issues in selection and training of local workers are presented as well as an introduction to the non-directive approach to community development. Writings based on rural case studies from various viewpoints are highlighted followed by a brief discussion of three prototypic projects. Next the cooperative extension approach to community development is analyzed; human relations training for community development is discussed; urban community development (among minorities in the United States) is mentioned; and related areas such as literacy, community schools, and indirect education are cited.

Batten

One writer who focuses on the local perspective is T. R. Batten. This British expert in community development is concerned with the human element at the local level in each of his four major books on community development. He is one of the most helpful sources in outlining the characteristics of facilitators whom he calls "community level workers."

Need for community education. According to Batten (1959) the community development movement is an outcome of the independence of European colonies after the Second World War. The colonial powers had introduced schools to produce local people to work for them as clerks, storekeepers, and administrators, and to teach the Christian religion. Since the purposes of schooling were Western purposes, schools in the colonies prepared young people for life outside their local communities. People inside those local communities came to fix their hopes on one or more of their children in the outside world, and on the school as the only means of preparing them for it. Correspondingly the school made more demands on the communities' children leaving them less time and energy to devote to education for life in the community (pp. 5-7).

With independence governments began to try to speed up the rate of development forcing people to adjust to rapid change and deal with problems for which schools did not prepare them. New methods and skills were necessary in order to grow more food, have better health, and possess more wealth. But getting people to adopt practices such as contour farming and fertilizing was difficult. Such adoption involved processes which neither the schools nor traditional education dealt with (Batten, 1959, p. 9).

> Community education is needed for yet another reason. People who have some basic values in common, respect for one another, and to some extent feel responsible for each other's welfare, can usually achieve a reasonably happy and satisfying community life together, even if they are poor and not very well educated (Batten, 1959, p. 9).

Community education is needed in such communities to strengthen the feeling of belonging and encourage ways of working together for the common good.

Batten maintains that the western style school was encouraging "an unregulated individualism which is destructive of the best elements of communal life." He pointed out that the school tends to weaken social bonds, to undermine the traditions, affections, and restraints that unite men with one another and generation with generation. Community education was needed to maintain and develop the forces which underlie positive community life while helping people to adjust to change.

The policies which national governments have developed to deal with such problems are generally known as community development policies. Community development seeks to insure that the effect of large-scale development will benefit the people. "At its simplest, it does this by stimulating people to discuss their problems, clarify their wants, and decide what they themselves can do to satisfy them (Batten, 1959, p. 13)."

> The trouble is that people must be stimulated, helped, and educated where they live, and that most of them live in quite small communities which are often hard to reach from a town, especially during the rainy season when some of them cannot be reached at all (Batten, 1959, p. 21).

Community development defined. In the very broadest sense community development includes almost anything that anyone may do to influence people's values, ideas, attitudes, relationships, or behavior for the better. It includes both social work and informal education from Batten's point of view. He defines community work as "any and every organized attempt to encourage, educate, influence, or help people to become actively involved in meeting some of their own needs (Batten, 1965, p. vii)."

Case study approach. By teaching a course of advanced training in community development for eighteen years at the University of London, Batten has accumulated a large number of case studies on community development problems. Thirty-seven of the cases are presented in The

<u>Human Factor in Community Work</u>. Each case study consists of an intro-
duction, the case, discussion of the case, and implications. The cases are
grouped under eight topic areas: meeting requests for help, suggesting
community projects, introducing improvements, establishing groups, working
with groups, working with leaders, dealing with faction, and asking for help.
Between three and seven cases are presented under each topic area. General
conclusions and implications are then presented to summarize each topic
area.

   Under the topic area, establishing groups, three conclusions are
specified:

> (a) people will not agree to form a group unless they
> believe that it will meet some need or serve some
> purpose of their own; (b) people will not continue to
> support a group unless it meets, and goes on meeting,
> some need or purpose of their own; and (c) when
> forming a group the worker needs to be able to anticipate
> whatever major difficulties the group may subsequently
> have to face and also how its members can be helped
> to avoid or overcome them (Batten, 1965, pp. 88-89).

   Under the topic area, meeting requests for help, the implications
advanced include:

> Situation One: The people or their representatives state
> a problem and seek the worker's advice as to how to
> meet it. Suggested order of work:
> (a) Investigate with the people the exact nature
>   of their problem.
> (b) Pool with them ideas as to possible solutions.
> (c) Encourage and help them to investigate the
>   advantages and disadvantages of each with a
>   view to deciding which solution is most acceptable
>   and practical for them.

(d) Leave the final decision entirely to them.

(e) Help them to obtain any technical advice they
    may need while they are reaching their decision,
    or afterwards while they are implementing it
    (Batten, 1965, p. 23).

In the concluding paragraph of his book of case studies, Batten argues that there is a universality of community development problems. He maintains that the conclusions "are likely to be relevant for community workers everywhere (Batten, 1965, p. 184)."

Training for community development. After reviewing a variety of experts' opinions on the qualifications needed by a village worker, Batten concludes:

> All this makes a formidable list of requirements,
> especially when it is remembered that all this
> knowledge, all these technical, teaching, and human
> relations skills, and all these personal qualities are
> demanded of the poorest paid and lowest level of
> field worker. No newly recruited worker can possibly
> have them all. He has to be trained, and how to train
> him most effectively is still one of the major problems,
> if not the major problem, of the organizers of community
> development work (Batten, 1962, p. 6).

Batten addresses the problem of training.

Selection is the first issue considered. An interesting selection process for village workers employed in India is described. Applicants are tested individually on their abilities to learn certain skills and to communicate them to villagers. The applicants' attitudes towards menial tasks are tested. The selection process includes a 10-mile walking trip and a 15-mile bicycle trip.

It includes a test of ability to take comprehensive notes and carry an oral message correctly. It also includes observation of applicants in a variety of situations: under conditions of emergency, organizing entertainment for rural people, and responding to an interview (Batten, 1962, p. 26).

In subsequent chapters Batten discusses general issues related to training professional and non-professional workers, problems of organization and method, discussion, finding content, getting participation, developing skill, and meeting individual needs. Although some of the discussion is related only to professional agents, many of the issues are relevant to the facilitator role as outlined in this study.

Although he supports the idea of a facilitator, Batten (1965) recognizes one problem. If a villager serving as a facilitator among peers makes a mistake, a loss of confidence by the villagers may render the facilitator ineffective. A village worker from the outside can be moved to another village and start again with little problem. But the facilitator is a member of the community and must live with the mistake (p. 2).

The non-directive approach. One of Batten's (1967) ideas which has a high degree of appropriateness to the facilitator idea is the non-directive approach in community and group work. The theory behind this approach is that people are more likely to' act on what they themselves have freely decided to do than on what a worker has tried to convince them they ought to do (p. v).

The directive approach, far more common, leads a worker to try to gain acceptance from clients as a person whose advice is worth having and whose opinions are worth listening to. This type of person works as a leader of groups and as the counsellor of those who have problems. A worker-client relationship is built in. The directive approach has been used extensively in meeting people's material needs. It has limitations, however, in meeting people's psychological needs. People tend to sense, resent, and resist direct attempts to influence them. Often the only effect of the directive approach is the reverse of what the agent intended (Batten, 1967, pp. 5-10).

In contrast,

> Workers who adopt the non-directive approach no longer try to guide or persuade. They stimulate people to think about their needs, feed in information about possible ways of meeting them, and encourage them to decide for themselves what they will do to meet them.

Thus they aim at stimulating a process of self-determination and self-help. They aim to encourage people to develop themselves by thinking and acting for themselves (Batten, 1967, pp. v & 11).

Batten (1967) lists four potential advantages of this approach: (a) it enables leaders to accomplish more with their limited resources; (b) it helps develop people; (c) it helps the emergence of solidarity; and (d) it provides many opportunities for educating and influencing people. The approach is usually chosen because an individual or agency has more needs than it could possibly

hope to meet out of its own unaided resources, or because the people's greatest
need is to acquire more confidence and competence in acting for themselves
(pp. 15, 16 & 27).

According to Batten (1967) there are seven stages in which a group may
find itself ranging from "vaguely dissatisfied but passive" to "satisfied with
the result of what they have achieved." He describes how, by using the non-
directive approach, a worker can stimulate awareness, desire for change,
consideration of courses of action, organization, detailed planning, and
readjustment due to developments, in a group. Using non-directive methods
has been proven productive in many situations both in developing and developed
countries (pp. 47 & 95).

In summary, although Batten's concept of a community level worker is
one of a professional outsider, sensitivity to local individuals, processes,
and priorities, is emphasized. Also Batten's definition of community work
embraces both development and education integrating both in the same activities.
Batten's philosophy is strong in diverse geographical areas and his influence
is apparent in programs not associated with him.

Rural Community Development Case Studies

India. Readings on community development in India, published by the
Council of Social Development (1970), show considerable complementarity
with Batten's ideas. The Council, set up by the India International Centre

in 1964, focuses primarily on national development. When the local level is considered, the bias is towards outside intervention by experts. Discussion only occasionally centers on characteristics of village level workers and then particular skills, knowledge, and attitudes, are implicit rather than explicit. However, the diversity of activities and scope of viewpoints provides some interesting insights.

Willner (1970), writing for the Council, mentions that a community agent may represent a new factor in the life of the community, competing with established leaders in various activities. She recommends that established leaders be located, that the source and nature of their authority be identified, that the extent of their influence be determined, and that their cooperation or neutrality be gained (pp. 88-89).

A discussion of problem areas in community development contributes to the usefulness of the Council's approach in the improvement of the facilitator idea. Some of the problems are: (a) the philosophy of community development may come to be remote from village realities; (b) an overemphasis on construction leads to neglect of self-development and self-determination; (c) people must be made conscious of their rights and responsibilities as citizens; (d) development officials should promote solidarity as well as leadership or factions may divide the village and local leaders fail to promote village development; (e) emphasis on centrally directed activities runs

counter to the explicit demands for public initiative and cooperation at the
local level; (f) benefits of community development may accrue mainly to the
better-situated segments of village society intensifying inequalities;
(g) voluntary agencies and their workers should strengthen existing institutions
rather than creating other institutions; and (h) progress must be made to
relieve the burden of paper work and other bureaucratic activities which
hamper village development (Council, 1970, pp. 181-186).

King. Another case study book is King's Working with People in
Community Action which is fairly general and uncomplicated. Because of
its readability, it would make a useful training tool especially in raising basic
issues in community development. Chapter eight deals with training, especially
the use of case studies in preparing community workers. Other chapters
present "how to" vignettes dealing with felt needs, catalysts, committees,
and community councils.

The most useful part of King's casebook to this study of facilitator
characteristics is the discussion of "indirect leadership," a concept close to
Batten's non-directive approach. Since the characteristics of this kind of
leadership improve on Batten's presentation, they are worth noting:

> Indirect leadership lacks the element of recognized
> responsibility. It works quietly, behind the scenes,
> through others. It is skillful in its choice of direct
> leaders. It receives neither credit nor blame. It
> accepts no formal office. Indirect leadership has
> broad vision and purpose and is more lasting in time.
> Without the power and prestige which attach to official

position, the indirect leader provides inspiration,
guidance, energy, and frequently co-ordination to
direct leaders in functional groups (King, 1965,
p. 75).

Biddle. Unlike previous authors using case studies, Biddle presents

two extended case studies with more thorough discussion. One of the cases

is rural, the other is urban. Based on the case studies, a number of

assumptions are set forth which are worth mentioning:

(a) Each person is valuable, unique, and capable of
growth toward greater social sensitivity and responsibility. Each person has underdeveloped abilities in
initiative, originality, and leadership. These qualities
can be cultivated and strenghened.

These abilities tend to emerge and grow stronger
when people work together in small groups that serve
the common (community) good.

There will always be conflicts between persons
and factions. Properly handled, the conflicts can be
used creatively. Agreement can be reached on specific
next steps of improvement, without destroying philosophic
or religious differences.

Although the people may express their differences
freely, when they become responsible they often choose
to refrain in order to further the interest of the whole
group and of their idea of community.

People will respond to an appeal to altruism as well
as an appeal to selfishness. These generous motivations
may be used to form groups that serve an inclusive
welfare of all people in a community. Groups are capable
of growth toward self-direction when the members assume
responsibility for group growth and for an inclusive local
welfare.

(b) Human beings and groups have both good and bad
impulses. Under wise encouragement they can strengthen
the better in themselves and help others to do likewise.

When the people are free of coercive pressures, and
can then examine a wide range of alternatives, they tend
to choose the ethically better and the intelligently wiser
course of action.

> There is satisfaction in serving the common
> welfare, even as in serving self-interest. A concept
> of the common good can grow out of group experience
> that serves the welfare of all in some local area. This
> sense of responsibility and belonging can be strengthened
> even for those to whom community is least meaningful.
> (c) Satisfaction and self-confidence gained from small
> accomplishments can lead to the undertaking of more and
> more difficult problems, in a process of continuing growth.
> (d) Within the broad role of community developer, there
> are several subroles to be chosen, depending upon the
> developer's judgment of the people's needs:
>> Encourager, friend,
>> Objective observer, analyst
>> Participant in discussion
>> Participant in some action
>> Process expert, adviser
>> Flexible adjuster to varying needs for prominence
> (Biddle, 1965, pp. 65-72).

Biddle's assumptions are quite close to the Ecuador Project's assumptions

regarding facilitators although the latter's assumptions are not so explicit.

Biddle adds to the facilitator idea with his description of a similar type

of individual whom he calls "the encourager." Not an inventor, nor an

introducer, nor a promoter of new ideas, the encourager is an instigator of

processes that call upon others to become innovators. The encourager hopes

people will exercise more control over change rather than be victims of

change. To this end the encourager stimulates the expression of ideas, an

atmosphere of confidence, and an adherence to the good that can be shared by

everyone (Biddle, 1965, pp. 259-265).

In summary, Batten proposes the "village level worker" role and

elaborates many of the appropriate skills, knowledge areas, and attitudes for

such a worker. Case studies in India indicate issues related to basically the same village level worker. King talks of indirect leadership which is close to Batten's non-directive approach and which elaborates the community worker's role. Finally Biddle introduces "the encourager" emphasizing the process-related behaviors of the role which is slightly different yet complementary with Batten, King, and the Ecuador Project's facilitator concept.

In addition to the viewpoints of community development experts, reports of prototype organizations and projects are helpful in understanding the broad field of community development. Three prototypes are particularly interesting in relation to the facilitator idea.

Animation Rurale. A private French technical assistance society developed the concept of animation rurale. First applied in Morocco in 1956, it was transplanted to Senegal in 1959. Seeking to promote grassroots activity independent, where possible, of financial support from the government (Coombs, 1974, p. 72; Sheffield & Diejomaoh, 1972, p. 133).

> The essence of animation rurale--an amalgam of sociological and political concepts with a dash of economics--was that village peasants should be stimulated by one of their own number to identify and articulate their needs for improvement, to take initiatives to help themselves, and to demand from their central government and its various technical services the kinds of help they needed to reinforce their efforts, consistent with national goals and plans.

> The key change agents in this process--the animateurs-- would be farmers selected by their fellow villagers and given special training to serve as guide and stimulator for the village and also as liaison with outside sources of technical and material assistance (Coombs, 1974, p. 72).

The _animateurs_ in Senegal, local farmers selected through consultation with the villagers, are given intensive training in general civic duties, the meaning of national planning, methods of cooperative management, and technical innovations in agriculture and animal husbandry. They return to their villages to analyze village needs and problems, design local develop- ment activities, stimulate people's awareness of their collective capacity for self-improvement, and facilitate the activities of the government's technical- services agents. Although considerable success is achieved the movement often flounders due to a lack of sophisticated technical advice and more practical material follow-up. The _animateurs_, unfortunately, are isolated from each other and from the necessary support of the organization which trains them (Coombs, 1974, pp. 72-73).

Comilla. Established in 1959, the East Pakistan Academy for Rural Development, under Akhter Hameed Khan, developed an interesting experiment in rural development. Located at Comilla, the Academy is set up to operate as a semi-autonomous institution under a board of governors made up of ranking government officials involved in rural development. Employing the central concept of assisting Bengali villagers by listening and learning from them, not by talking and instructing, the Comilla Project developed an approach, similar to extension education, in which much of the effort moves from the bottom up rather than from the top down (Raper, 1970, pp. vii & 12; Coombs, 1974, p. 85).

Although comprehensive in nature, the Comilla Project's relationship

with villages is an interesting comparison with similar relationships in the

Ecuador Project. The villagers choose one of their number to act as their

educational liaison with the outside world, including the Academy. The

participating villages agree to:

> (a) organize themselves, choose a chairman and
> become a registered cooperative society; (b) hold
> weekly meetings, with compulsory attendance of
> all members; (c) select a man from the group and
> send him to the Academy once a week for training
> so that he could be the organizer and teacher of the
> group; (d) keep proper and complete records;
> (e) use supervised production credit; (f) adopt
> improved agricultural practices and skills;
> (g) make regular cash and in-kind savings deposits;
> (h) join the central cooperative association of the
> thana;[1] and (i) hold regular member education
> sessions (Coombs, 1974, p. 85).

In addition to the organizer, a similarly chosen "model farmer" becomes

a key agricultural teacher in his own community. The model farmer is a

resident village farmer selected by his cooperative; he spends one day each

week in training at the Academy in order to provide liaison between the

farmers and the Academy, and his role in the village includes that of

agricultural innovator. In early years, training included exposure to

cooperative practices, improved methods of cultivation, credit, capital forma-

tion by savings, joint use of agricultural implements, joint storage of water,

joint planning, formation of bullock groups, conduct of meetings, accounts keeping, and marketing of agricultural produce. As the cooperatives became more active, the duties of organizers and model farmers were combined in a paid manager (Rapper, 1970, pp. 51; Coombs, 1974, p. 85).

Coombs concludes that the Comilla Project has shown:

> that a two-way channel of educational communication between villagers and outside sources of knowledge and expertise--using as go-betweens teachers of their own choice in whom they had high confidence--can be more effective than the more familiar one-way, top-down extension model.

However, the greatest beneficiaries are the "better-off farmers (Coombs, 1974, p. 87)."

Vicos. An attempt in Peru to incorporate a community of Indians into a more modern way of life was instituted by Cornell University in cooperation with the Indigenous Institute of Peru and with the support of the Peruvian government. Using careful planning, program directors designed a modest program of technical assistance and education which had fairly wide acceptance and stimulated most community members to improve their lot through their own efforts. The goals are higher living standards, social respect, and a self-reliant and enlightened community. The program centers on three major areas of development: economics and technology, nutrition and health, and education. Later, social organization became a fourth area of concern. Taking their cue from community aspirations, program workers seek to form and strengthen local groups so that the people may acquire the knowledge, skills, and attitudes needed for self-reliant growth. At relatively small cost, the program indicates that the Indians, once given proper encouragement, advice, and respect, can do much by themselves to improve themselves (Dalton, 1971, pp. 530-564).

The program at Vicos can be criticized to some extent on its assumptions and reported outcomes. Education is largely understood in terms of school attendance; middlemen are promoted in marketing; and the increased acquisition of appliances is applauded. However, the nurturing of responsibility and initiative within the community, rather than importing alien and transitory institutions from without is relevant to the consideration of facilitator's roles in non-formal education.

All of these three case studies are interesting and relevant due to their emphasis on community organization to solve local educational and development problems. The project at Vicos demonstrates the feasibility of community self-improvement in an Andean culture. Here a project has apparently been able to respond to local aspirations even though project sponsorship is by a Northamerican university.

The Comilla project introduces the role of model farmers and managers selected by each local community. The organization of the project whereby local leaders are connected with support in the form of training and continuous information is a particularly helpful insight in improving the facilitator concept.

Finally the <u>animateur</u> role in <u>animation rurale,</u> less structured than the model farmer role in Comilla, is closer to the present facilitator role. An analysis of the problems of support for the <u>animateur</u> might guide the improvement of the facilitator idea in particular settings.

These case studies are often compared, in the literature on community development, to the cooperative extension education approach. Certainly a discussion of the important approaches to community development would be incomplete without a careful look at the extension philosophy, organization, and impact, as well as some adaptations of extension in different countries.

Extension Education

In terms of scope, philosophy, and organization, the cooperative extension education approach is so well developed as to comprise a category of its own. Some authors include it in nonformal education. For this study of facilitator characteristics it is considered under community development.

Coombs (1974) mentions the conventional extension model and discusses other versions found in Korea and Senegal. He finds a number of shortcomings in extension services: (a) extension is seen mainly as an informing and persuading process involving new technical practices; (b) often there is an "unfortunate bureaucratic isolation" from other agricultural services; (c) an authoritarian attitude is widespread among extension workers in local areas; (d) local extension workers often operate haphazardly with neither priorities nor plans; (e) they spread themselves too thin to be effective; (f) they often neglect smaller and subsistence farmers; (g) their recommendations are often standardized rather than responding specifically to individual needs; (h) their field agents' inservice training is often neglected; and (i) the local workers are often burdened with distracting chores (pp. 125-126; 239-240).

Menkerios (1972) also mentions a number of problems with the implementation of extension services (pp. 1-4 & 28-30). Apparently the extension education approach has been implemented in a large number of countries with varying results. However, the nature of extension education, its purposes, and its organization for leadership development are surveyed with findings relevant to this study.

The nature of extension education. Extension is defined as

> an informal education process which aims to teach
> rural people how to improve their level of living by
> their own efforts, through making wise use of natural
> resources at their disposal in better systems of farming
> and homemaking, for the benefit of the individual, the
> family, the community and the nation (Bradfield, 1966,
> p. 11).

The Extension Service in the United States intends to promote:

> (a) greater ability in maintaining more efficient farms
> and better homes; (b) greater ability in acquiring higher
> incomes and levels of living on a continuing basis;
> (c) increased competency and willingness, by both
> adults and youth, to assume leadership and citizenship

responsibilities; and (d) increased ability and
willingness to undertake organized group action
when such will contribute effectively to improving
their welfare (Subcommittee on Scope, 1958, p. 3).

In order to achieve those goals, extension cooperates with political parties,

community and social development agencies, veterinary and forestry services,

health services, educational services, and marketing services (Bradfield,

1966, pp. 15-17).

Careful planning and program building are characteristic of extension.

Workers are encouraged to develop clear written objectives and translate

them into written programs to ensure continuity and to provide a basis of

cooperation. In planning, they are directed to study the situation and the

facts, define the problem, consider the possibilities, anticipate outcomes,

and develop a flexible work outline. Evaluation is another important

component of extension (Bradfield, 1966, pp. 126-138).

Knaus (1955) outlines program building principles for extension

education:

1. People who benefit by a program should assist
   in its development.
2. Base problems on needs determined by analysis
   of facts in the situation.
3. Objectives and solutions must offer satisfaction.
4. Permanence with flexibility facilitate operations.
5. Balance with emphasis gives direction.
6. A definite plan of action is part of program.
7. It must start where the people are.
8. Evaluation of results should guide revisions.
9. Program making is a continuous process, a teaching
   process, and a coordinating process (p. 29).

The areas of program emphasis mentioned are:

> (a) efficiency in agricultural production; (b) efficiency
> in marketing, distribution, and utilization; (c) conserva-
> tion, development, and use of natural resources;
> (d) management on the farm and in the home; (e) family
> living; (f) youth development; (g) leadership development;
> (h) community improvement and resource development; and
> (i) public affairs (Subcommittee on Scope, 1958, pp. 8-12).

The extension approach assumes five stages in the acceptance of a new idea: awareness, interest, evaluation, trial, and adoption. All clients of extension are assumed to pass through each of the stages. This acceptance process is a basis for planning extension programs and selecting appropriate extension methods (Bradfield, 1966, p. 29). Spector (1971), however, maintains that adoption of an innovation must be viewed as an interactive process. He feels that it is impossible to prescribe adoption by characteristics of adopters or by practices employed (p. 46).

Extension leaders. There are a variety of leadership roles cited in extension literature. Some of the functions of voluntary and professional leaders mentioned are:

> (a) stimulating people in the community to do the
> actual recruiting; (b) helping the local people define
> the type of leadership needed for specific jobs;
> (c) serving as organizer and coordinator in the
> indirect recruiting process; (d) helping local people
> think through desirable characteristics of a leader;
> (There is no one list of characteristics that will
> insure success. In general, a person who is respected,
> liked, congenial, interested, willing, mature,
> intelligent and cooperative is more likely to succeed

than one who is weak in one or more of these traits);
(e) carrying on a good public relations program which
provides the community with information about the 4-H
program and 4-H leadership; and (f) maintaining good
relationships with groups and institutions having an
interest in the community (Missouri Extension Service,
1968, p. 6).

The 4-H project leader's role is perhaps the closest to the Ecuadorian

facilitator. This leader's role is to work closely with 4-H members to help

them to learn by doing. Leaders may or may not have some knowledge of

the project in which they are involved. Many leaders "have learned along

with the members in the beginning projects (Lindsay, 1972, p. 4)."

In summary knowledge and skills needed by extension personnel include:

(a) knowledge of group organization, leadership development and evaluation;

(b) understanding of human relations, group dynamics, and the needs of

leaders; (c) understanding of needs and interests of youth and adults;

(d) ability to communicate, motivate, and find and use available resources;

and (e) ability to recruit, teach, and give recognition to leaders. The basic

assumptions about extension leadership are:

(a) people are benefited by serving in leadership roles;
(b) people are available for leadership jobs and will
devote adequate time to receive knowledge and develop
necessary skills; (c) people are capable of performing
leadership functions; (d) leadership skills and roles are
specific to the job or group where leadership is needed;
(e) experience received in positions of leadership in 4-H
will help to prepare a person for other leadership roles
in Extension and the community; (f) leadership development is a continuous and gradual process--the best

> learning comes through doing; (g) leadership develop-
> ment is dependent on and contributes to other phases
> of extension programming such as program develop-
> ment and staff training; and (h) the effectiveness of
> extension personnel is expanded and multiplied through
> the help of volunteer leadership (Missouri Extension
> Service, 1968, pp. 3-4).

This discussion of extension education, however, is based on the program

which has evolved in the United States. A look at Extension in other countries,

beyond the general criticism of Coombs and Menkerios, is useful.

Other extension programs. In a comparative survey of agricultural

extension education systems, Axinn and Thorat (1972) analyze extension in

twelve countries. Their conclusions are: (a) change in a group is directly

related to communication with the outside world; (b) success of an extension

program depends on the extent to which its benefit to farmers is immediate

and high, cost to them is low, recommended practices are relatively simple

and easily tested; (c) the effectiveness of extension agents varies inversely

with the social distance from their clients; (d) "first line workers" should be

local workers selected by the group to be served; (e) the clientele must have

confidence in local workers; and (f) local workers should employ multiple

communication methods (p. 189).

Jones (1974) holds the opinion that extension workers should make

their own responsibilities clear to learners in order to prevent dependency

relationships from developing. He also notes, "Expecting a farmer to maximize profit is unrealistic when he is concerned with presenting himself in the community as farming in a way considered proper for his status (pp. 34-35)."

The extension approach emphasizes local initiative and strives to connect clients to sources of information usually through governmental agencies. Also emphasized, particularly in relation to local leaders' roles, are communication skills, ability to motivate, group dynamics, and understanding of human relations. Other groups and organizations are also interested in these areas. Most of those groups focus, to some degree, on the human relations aspect.

Human Relations

Some organizations have introduced human relations training into their community development activities. Drawing inspiration and experience from T-groups, values clarification, and motivational training, these organizations focus on leadership development.

Peace Corps. This organization provides varied insights into the improvement of the facilitator idea. The experiential training approach supported by the Peace Corps is learner centered rather than subject centered. It is structured to achieve active rather than passive learner responsibility and involvement in the learning process.

Peace Corps' reliance on small groups is mirrored in the technical descriptions of a number of sophisticated modifications of the small-group discussion. Although certain of the groups described may not be appropriate to more unsophisticated facilitators, the Ecuador Project confirms the assertion that:

> The most effective way to achieve a climate of support, experimentation, problem-solving, and assessment of experience is through the use of small groups, where a level of trust can develop that is difficult to achieve in a larger community (Wight & Hammons, 1970, p. 119).

A brief description of Batten's non-directive approach as well as a variety of techniques and exercises to promote leadership, group dynamics, and an understanding of human relations, as well as an excellent bibliography are included by Wight and Hammons in Guidelines for Peace Corps Cross-Cultural Training (1970). Particular aspects of this source are already used in facilitator training in Ecuador.

National Training Laboratories (NTL). Nylen's Handbook of Staff Development and Human Relations Training (1967), like the Peace Corps Guidlines mentioned above, is a practical guide to the philosophy and techniques developed by NTL for use in Africa. Nylen mentions a number of task roles which may be relevant to facilitators: initiating activity, seeking information, seeking opinion, giving information, giving opinion, elaborating, coordinating, and summarizing. A separate list of roles, called group building and maintenance roles, includes encouraging, gatekeeping, standard setting, following, and expressing group feeling. Roles which involve both task and maintenance are evaluating, diagnosing, testing for consensus, mediating, and relieving tension. A fourth list of "types of non-functional behavior" is also enumerated (pp. 68-69).

Exercises designed to help individuals and groups acquire skills to effectively assume the roles mentioned are outlined by Nylen (1967). Some of the more interesting exercises provide practice in dealing with an angry person, understanding hidden motives, utilizing group resources, and involving another person.

Motivational training. U.S.A.I.D. supports motivational training in Guatemala, Panama and Ecuador. Regular use of NTL laboratory methods at Loyola University became the stimulus for Guatemalan graduates to encourage U.S.A.I.D. to duplicate the Loyola program in their country. U.S.A.I.D. supports a Guatemalan institution that contracts for services as local trainers. The trainers are prepared at a six-week experience in Puerto Rico in a limited number of laboratory situations. T-group techniques, problem-solving techniques, and organization development are learned by the trainers (American Technical Assistance Corp., 1971, pp. ii-iii & 11).

Although limited conclusions can be drawn from a few years of activities, a number of recommendations for improvement are made in an evaluation study. However, the general conclusion is that motivational training produces, among participants, a belief in the possibility of accelerating development through group self-help efforts. Furthermore, this belief frequently leads to actions "that assist achievement of national development goals (American Technical Assistance Corp., 1971, p. i).

Peace Corps experiences, NTL materials, and motivational training experiments, are all relevant to the facilitator idea. Since the sources are limited in number and appear to be strongly dependent on particular settings, their utility to facilitators will depend considerably on specific facilitator settings.

Urban Community Development

Likewise the literature on this subject, relevant to the facilitator idea, is relatively scarce. Also dependent on particular settings community development in urban areas does provide new insights.

Though community development began with a rural emphasis, its application in urban environments has tended to bring out other areas of emphasis. Much of the literature is concerned with social welfare, legal awareness, and political organization. However the outside intervention bias has remained a feature, to a large extent, of urban as well as rural community development.

Brager and Purcell (1967) present a series of readings from the "mobilization experience." One of the readings addresses the issue of non-professional helpers. Visiting homemakers are recruited to act in a helping role with low-income women. Their social distance from the clients is much less than that of the professional staff members of the organization (Mobilization for Youth). The visiting homemakers are selected on the basis of their warmth, friendliness, understanding, and skills in various areas of home management.

> The homemakers were untrained, but they were not unskilled. As we have suggested, they had considerable ability to cope with their environment and therefore much to offer clients who were less resourceful than they (p. 190).

The "visiting homemaker" case study concludes that indigenous staff can make an invaluable contribution to a social agency's efforts to help low-income clients provided that the staff are engaged in ways to realize their potential. They are very effective in providing clients with skills to cope with difficult management problems (Brager & Purcell, 1967, pp. 206-207).

In another reading on indigenous staff it is pointed out that hiring local non-professionals has been undertaken in education, medicine, mental health, and recreation as well as social work. In some cases non-proessionals who are hired overcome their own problems (e.g., delinquency) as a result of their work (Brager & Purcell, 1967, pp. 212-219).

Leadership appears to develop through the act of leading. "The art of leadership training may lie in providing just the right roles to stimulate the emergence of more and more leadership." The idea then, "is to restructure the groups so that different members play the helper role at different times (Brager & Purcell, 1967, pp. 222-223). However also observed is that in developing a group of indigenous non-professionals an outgroup orientation may affect the new staff's perceptions in a way that skews them toward the middle class (Brager & Purcell, 1967, p. 215).

Another enlightening source is The Organizer's Manual. This "movement" handbook provides very practical suggestions for organization and activism. Topics covered, among others, are: planning for the first meeting, fundraising, teach-ins, workshops and study groups, and guerrilla theater. There is also some discussion of self-education as it relates to increasing one's political consciousness, analyzing "your opposition and society," and developing the political consciousness of the group. This book also features an extensive and practical bibliography.

Community Development Related Areas

A large variety of subject matter areas could be relevant to the facilitator idea depending on the specific setting and the objectives of the facilitator's community. Three such areas which relate to community development are literacy, community schools, and indirect education.

Literacy. This topic is certainly important to community development.
Freire and Ashton-Warner, two authorities on literacy, are included in the
discussion of non-formal education and the Ecuador Project. Other sources
are often too technical or promote a highly formalized methodology which
is of very doubtful relevance for facilitators. Laubach (1960), however, has
developed a method called "each one teach one" which has been tried in a
majority of the countries of the world. Its simplicity, the emphasis on
building confidence in the learner, and the reading materials developed in
the approach are all potentially relevant to facilitators.

Community Schools. An appealing idea is presented by Houghton and
Tregear (1969): the school as an educational institution may be based on
purely educational criteria. It could be an instrument for local and national
development providing education and training for community members outside
the normal school age. This type of school would be attended, supported,
and understood by all members of the community. It would feature learning
in "natural" settings. Examples of such schools in operation around the
world are given. Piveteau (1972) discusses the well elaborated ecole de
promotion collective, a community school approach in Francophone Africa.

Batten (1959) is also interested in community schools. He sees the
classroom moving to the community. He also advocates teaching skills
useful in community life.

Indirect Education. Related to his feelings about community schools, Batten (1959) believes that in order to have a lasting influence on the children the school must also influence their parents (p. 74). Etling (1972) also mentions the use of indirect education in Bolivia. Nutrition practices are taught to parents through elementary school classes for their children (pp. 160-161). Indirect education might be a useful approach for facilitators as well.

Although practical application to the facilitator idea is unclear, urban community development, literacy education, community schools, and indirect education all provide ways of integrating education and development. All of these areas tend to view the community as a classroom.

These last three community development related areas bring attention back to an institution which has been omnipresent yet only tangentially treated in this study. That institution is the school. A discriminating look at teacher effectiveness will provide even more understanding of the potential of the facilitator of NFE.

Teacher Effectiveness

The literature on teacher effectiveness is voluminous. That which relates to the facilitator idea as defined by the study, however, is much more limited. Beginning with a look at a current phenomenon, improving university teaching, which cuts across many concerns of teacher effectiveness, this section reviews instruments developed to observe classroom interaction, the competency-based education movement, literature dealing with helping relationships in education, leadership and management theory, and the ideas of certain activist educators. Sources in these areas contribute insights into improving the facilitator concept. Many of the skills, knowledge areas, and attitudes relevant to facilitators are also mentioned.

Improving University Teaching

In his 1974 doctoral thesis, Melnik surveys a vast quantity of research on teacher effectiveness in order to develop his Student Centered Analysis of Teaching, a list of variables which seem to determine teaching effectiveness. Over a two-year period, those variables have evolved into a list of characteristics called "teaching analysis by students (TABS)."

The TABS are thirty-nine statements of teachers' behaviors. They are used as a part of the Clinic to Improve University Teaching at the University of Massachusetts. Teachers who seek the Clinic's services are videotaped by Clinic technicians and rated by the students in their class. The rating consists of an examination of the TABS items by each student followed by one of five responses:

(a) No improvement is needed (very good or excellent performance);
(b) Little improvement is needed (generally good performance);
(c) Improvement is needed (generally mediocre performance);
(d) Considerable improvement is needed (generally poor performance);
(e) Not a necessary skill or behavior for this course (Clinic, 1973).

The students' ratings are then compared to the videotape by a Clinic diagnostician in the presence of the teacher in order to observe weaknesses and develop strategies for improvement. A number of the TABS items are relevant to the facilitator role and are included in the findings.

The TABS is actually a modified observation instrument. Unlike most standard observation instruments, ratings do not take place during the inter-action observed. Rather the students rate the teacher based on their memories of the teacher's performance related to each item. A survey of selected observation instruments is appropriate to more fully understand the TABS. An examination of observation instruments is also useful as a source of possible facilitator skills, knowledge, and attitudes.

Observation instruments

Simon and Boyer (1967) analyze twenty-six classroom observation instruments. The instruments are for interaction analysis sytems which "are 'shorthand' methods for collecting observable objective data about the way people talk and act (p. 1). " One finding is that "Very few of the cognitive systems can be coded 'live' in the classroom, " since coding is sufficiently complex to require both tape recordings and tapescripts of the classroom interaction be used for analysis (p. 11). Coding complexity is one of the reasons why the use of many of the systems "has never extended beyond the researcher who developed them (pp. 11-13)." In addition to degree of complexity there is concern about the number of coders needed to record observations, special hardware (audiotaping and videotaping equipment) required, and the ease with which the categories could be unambiguously and exclusively identified. Obviously, these factors limit the usefulness of the instruments in facilitator settings to a greater degree than in classroom settings.

The idea of observation instruments, however, is compelling. Simon and Boyer (1967) feel that observation instruments have the potential to provide objective data necessary for research, teacher training, and super-vision. "Even in widely divergent circumstances. . . teacher behaviors do not appear to change in different settings nor with different pupils (p. 18)." The instruments are regarded as very useful in giving feedback to teachers about their own teaching behavior and in helping to promote pupil growth if used in the classroom. These conslusions are equally valid for facilitators of non-formal education.

Two of the more promising instruments available are examined in more detail. Amidon provides a list of ten categories for interaction analysis: accepts feeling, praises or encourages, accepts or uses ideas of students, asks questions, lecturers, gives directions, criticizes or justifies authority, responds to student talk, initiates student talk, and silence or confusion. The categories are discussed and elaborated, in general terms. Most of the categories are incorporated into the list of the findings of the study. However, the generality of the categories limits their practicality until they are operationalized into specific behavioral statements.

The "Stanford Teacher Competence Appraisal Guide" provides seventeen categories entitled aims, planning, performance, evaluation, and community and professional. As with Amidon, the observer can only produce highly subjective data unless the categories are translated into behavioral statements.

Hamachek (1969) is yet more general. He lists four dimensions of teacher personality and behavior: (a) personal characteristics; (b) instructional procedures and interaction styles; (c) perceptions of self; and (d) perceptions of others.

Although not tied to a particular classroom observation instrument, Schmuck and Schmuck (1971) devote considerable attention to interaction analysis. Their approach is to look at the classroom in terms of group dynamics theory. An assumption made is that cohesive groups are more concerted in their goal direction than are non-cohesive groups. Next, leadership is considered in its impact on group processes. An observation list for goal-directed leadership is included (p. 42). Also discussed are levels of communication skills including another observation sheet (p. 100). A brief review of theories of group development follows.

Six "salient characteristics" of school organizations which may directly affect classroom group processes are outlined: (a) trust and openness; (b) skills of constructive openness; (c) influence positions of teachers; (d) orientations to human motivation; (e) leadership role of the principal; and (f) student observations of the faculty. These general organizational characteristics are relevant to any organization supporting facilitators, and, to some extent, facilitators themselves.

Schmuck and Schmuck (1971) include discussion, techniques, and exercises aimed at improving each of the topics discussed in the book. Their general approach to improving skills, as opposed to the individual observation instruments, is a problem-solving sequence which includes (a) a statement of the problem, (b) diagnosis by means of a force field, (c) brainstorming to find alternative actions, (d) designing concrete plans of action (including the observation instruments), and (e) trying out the plan through a simulated activity (pp. 142-143).

There is considerable relationship between the TABS, the observation instruments, and competency-based education. All are approaches to improving certain behaviors by defining the behaviors then observing them as they are used in an actual situation. However competency-based education is far more elaborate than this.

Competency-Based Education (CBE)

An examination of the characteristics of CBE in terms of their applicability to the facilitator idea proves interesting. Elam establishes three levels of characteristics of competency-based teacher education.

Essential elements--
(a) Teaching competencies to be demonstrated are role-derived, specified in behavioral terms, and made public.
(b) Assessment criteria are competency-based, specify mastery levels, and made public.
(c) Assessment requires performance as prime evidence, takes student knowledge into account.
(d) Student's progress rate depends on demonstrated competency.
(e) Instructional program facilitates development and evaluation of specific competencies.

Implied Characteristics--
(a) Individualization.
(b) Feedback.
(c) Systemic program.
(d) Exit requirement emphasis.
(e) Modularization.
(f) Student and program accountability

Related, Desirable Characteristics--
(a) Field setting.
(b) Broad base for decision making.
(c) Protocol and training materials.
(d) Student participation in decision making.
(e) Research-oriented and regenerative.
(f) Career-continuous.
(g) Role integration (Elam, 1971, p. 6-11).

A comparison of Elam's characteristics with the preferred dimensions of NFE indicates considerable complementarity at least on a theoretical level. Both NFE and CBE favor individualized approaches and considerable program flexibility. Both are concerned with developing competencies through skill training as well as attention to knowledge and attitudes of learners. Both are concerned with education which is practical and applicable to learners' life needs and work needs. CBE is not without apparent weaknesses which are well documented by critics of the competency-based approach. Yet the potential of the competency-based approach to the facilitator is promising.

In one sixth cycle Teacher Corps project, thirteen "minimal competencies for teaching interns" are employed. Those which appear to have relevance for facilitators are: (a) exhibits change agent skills in the community; (b) uses a variety of techniques to improve learning; (c) can design, implement, and evaluate learning modules; (d) uses acquired competencies in community-based activities; (e) demonstrates management techniques; (f) can articulate personal goals; and (g) demonstrates competency in using resources (University of Massachusetts Teacher Corps, 1973, p. 2). Completion criteria for each of the competencies are indicated.

A second Teacher Corps project involving the development of team leaders specifies competencies for the leaders. Since the project is as concerned with the impact on the community as the impact on the school, the ramifications for facilitators are extensive. Five general roles for the team leaders are identified: (a) planning for team involvement; (b) fostering community interaction; (c) developing teaching skills; (d) fostering skills of analysis in teaching; and (e) counseling and advising. Competencies are discussed for fostering change, skills training, consultation, organizational development, interpersonal communications and influence, initiating structure and consideration, maintenance and task functions, problem solving, and systematic planning and implementation (Team Leadership Development Project, 1971). The specific competencies relevant to the facilitator idea are included in the findings of this study of facilitator characteristics.

CBE observation instruments, and the TABS, however, concentrate on educators' skills and neglect their attitudes. To compensate for this deficiency and more fully relate the impact of teacher effectiveness to facilitators of NFE, other perspectives are important. A relatively large body of literature on helping relationships of educators emphasizes attitudes. Much of this literature also deals with skills and knowledge.

Helping Relationships

This category of literature includes sources which focus more on the learning function than on the teaching function. The educator is viewed more as a facilitator of learning processes than as a classroom teacher.

Helping Relationships by Combs, Avila, & Purkey (1973) is devoted to "basic concepts for the helping professions." Apart from the early chapters, which deal with professionalism, psychology, and philosophy, insights useful to facilitators are given. Learning to listen is discussed as is developing

sensitivity. Suggestions for developing sensitivity include receptive observa-

tion, attempting artistic productions, writing personal documents, participating

in projective tests, and sensitivity training.

Combs, et al (1973), present a discussion of establishing helping

relationships which is particularly instructive. The authoritarian, laissez-

faire, and democratic approaches to helping are discussed. Groups operating

under authoritarian leadership are very efficient in carrying out tasks but

become confused when the authoritarian leaders leaves the group. The

laissez-faire group members are characterized by frustration, discontent,

and boredom. They have no models to emulate and receive no help. "As a

consequence, such groups soon disintegrate with little or nothing accomplished

(p. 211)." The democratic organizational structure is generally most pro-

ductive. "Participants become more involved and creative, and are generally

more interested and willing to take more active responsibility (p. 211)."

In describing their "helper" Combs et al (1973), might as well have been

writing about an effective facilitator:

> The helper does not devote his energies primarily to
> the diagnosis of problems and the formulation of
> answers to be applied to them. Instead, he actively
> involves himself in the processes of searching. He
> perceives his role as facilitator, helper, assister
> in a cooperative process of exploration and discovery.
> Problems are not approached from an external

138

> orientation; rather the helper "gets with it." He
> enters an encounter with his client or student that
> is designed between himself and his world. The
> Helper is less concerned with ultimate answers than
> with creating the conditions in which they can be most
> efficiently discovered. His expertise rests, not so
> much in knowing answers as in the process by which
> they may be brought into being.

> The helper operating in this frame of reference neither
> accepts responsibility for the solutions his client may
> arrive at nor for knowing what they "should be." He
> does accept responsibility for creating conditions which
> will be truly helpful in assisting the client's own search
> for self-fulfillment. To this end he enters a dialogue
> with him to seek effective solutions to problems and
> more adequate perceptions of self and the world (p. 313).

The helper is further discussed as a model to clients, as a reinforcer, and
as an extinguisher. Also discussed are: (a) limits in the helping relationships; (b) creating an atmosphere for change; (c) challenge and threat in the
atmosphere for change; (d) punishment and the helping relationship; and
(e) acceptance.

Finally, advice on helping through groups is useful. Conversation
groups, instruction groups, decision groups, and discovery groups are
mentioned as settings in which helping can occur (Coombs, et al., 1973,
pp. 279-283).

Rogers (1969) is concerned with experiential learning which he describes
as having a quality of personal involvement, as being self-initiated, as being
pervasive (making a difference in the behavior, the attitudes, or even the
personality of the learner), as being evaluated by the learner, and as having
its essence in meaning (to the learner) (p. 5). Qualities which facilitate

learning according to Rogers are: (a) realness in the facilitator of learning; (b) prizing, acceptance, trust; and (c) empathic understanding. Anticipating the cynics, Rogers presents "solid evidence" for his position.

Building on his title, <u>Freedom to Learn,</u> Rogers (1969) suggests methods of building freedom: (a) building upon problems perceived as real; (b) providing resources; (c) using learning contracts; (d) dividing the group; (e) organizing facilitator-learning groups; (f) helping students to become inquirers; (g) using simulations; (h) employing encounter groups; and (i) enabling self-evaluation. When the leader concentrates on creating a facilitative climate, according to Rogers, he does not use a number of traditional methods.

> He does <u>not assign readings.</u> He does <u>not lecture or expound</u> (unless requested to). He does <u>not evaluate and criticize</u> unless a student wishes his judgment on a product. He does <u>not give required examinations.</u> He does <u>not take sole responsibility for grades</u> (p. 144).

A number of personal thoughts on teaching and learning are stated. They explain Rogers' (1969) assumptions about the facilitator idea in education (p. 152). From these assumptions then guidelines for facilitating learning are derived:

> (a) The facilitator has much to do with setting the initial mood or climate of the group or class experience.
> (b) The facilitator helps to elicit and clarify the purposes of the individuals in the class as well as the more general purposes of the group.
> (c) He relies upon the desire of each student to implement

those purposes which have meaning for him, as the
motivational force behind significant learning.
(d) He endeavors to organize and make easily
available the widest possible range of resources for
learning.
(e) He regards himself as a flexible resource to be
utilized by the group.
(f) In responding to expressions in the classroom group,
he accepts both the intellectual content and the emotionalized
attitudes, endeavoring to give each aspect the approximate
degree of emphasis which it has for the individual or the
group.
(g) As the acceptant classroom climate becomes established,
the facilitator is able increasingly to become a participant
learner, a member of the group, expressing his views as
those of one individual only.
(h) He takes the initiative in sharing himself with the
group--his feelings as well as his thoughts--in ways which
do not demand nor impose but represent simply a
personal sharing which students may take or leave.
(i) Throughout the classroom experience, he remains
alert to the expressions indicative of deep or strong
feelings.
(j) In his functioning as a facilitator of learning, the
leader endeavors to recognize and accept his own
limitations (pp. 164-166).

Complimenting Rogers is a 1973 dissertation on a facilitator process

for self-directed learning. Reisser (1973) observes:

In order to facilitate self-directed learning, a counselor
helps a student to (a) identify goals for himself; (b) plan
activities which work toward those goals; (c) plan ways
to evaluate progress; (d) take major responsibility for
his own growth (p. x).

She also points out that little is known about how to help the student become

more proficient at self-directed learning and, "Little is known about the

learning process itself, especially as it relates to non-classroom experiences

(p. 1)."

> The idea of a facilitation process implies that one
> person helps another. Learning how to learn is
> enhanced by communication and sharing. Initial
> interests can be transformed into satisfying learning
> projects through directed dialogue. A skillful,
> empathetic counselor can do things that bring students
> to an awareness of their own self-directing capabilities.
> It is important to emphasize the interpersonal dynamics
> involved in this process. Without people to use it, a
> learning theory is an abstruse set of assertions. While
> a theory can be used to program a teaching machine or
> a do-it-yourself manual, it cannot create the spark of
> excitement between student and sponsor when they
> embark upon a shared quest for knowledge (p. 185).

A facilitator is able to explore the individual background and learning style

of each student, to ask questions that increase awareness and learning

competence, and to provide on-going support and feedback.

Reisser (1973) examines the learning process and finds that a person

engaged in learning is essentially "questioning" the environment in three

major ways: (a) by clarifying a picture of some aspect of that person's

world; (b) by adding meaning to what is seen by looking at the causes and

effects and by relating explicit data to less obvious facts and concepts;

and (c) by combining statie patterns and dynamic relationships to build a

new arrangement of facts and ideas (pp. 187-188).

> New competencies are built by first observing
> others and receiving instruction; secondly, by
> planning and attempting to perform, and making
> adjustments in the light of feedback; thirdly, by
> improving through practice, growing more
> flexible and independent; and fourthly, by achieving
> high levels of efficiency and creativity and the
> ability to teach others (p. 189).

Other factors which facilitate learning are arousing interest, gaining competence to deal with new information, using conceptual organizers, using non-specific catalysts (open-ended questions), soliciting feedback, and practice (p. 189).

The facilitator role, then, is concerned with questioning, reflecting, and suggesting to help the student (a) select an area of interest; (b) clarify it, differentiate it or specify its sub-parts; (c) organize the parts into meaningful patterns; (d) translate the patterns into engagers--goal-oriented statements that imply a beginning point, a sense of direction, and an ending point; (e) synthesize a goal statement; (f) plan activities which aim at accomplishing goals; and (g) plan ways to evaluate progress (Reisser, 1973, p. 190).

Reisser (1973) then compares the characteristics of a self-actualizing person according to Maslow, Rogers, and McKinnon & Barron. From the synthesis of the three lists, guidelines for "self-directed learning facilitators" are derived. Categories of "responsiveness" mentioned are (a) efficient perception of reality, (b) abstract thinking ability, (c) hypothesis testing, (d) interest in the unknown, (e) elegance of expression, (f) acceptance of others, (g) adaptability and spontaneity, and (h) creativity. Categories of "responsibility" listed are (a) problem centering, (b) autonomy, (c) self-evaluation and detachment, (d) liking for order, (e) nonconformity, , and

(f) acceptance of self (pp. 254-257). The specific guidelines are included in the Preliminary List of Facilitator Characteristics in the findings of this study of facilitator characteristics of NFE.

Charnofsky (1971) is concerned with the idea of facilitating learning among the "powerless." Drawing heavily on Carl Rogers, this author feels that prizing the learner is one of the most important activities of a facilitator. He is also concerned with understanding the target population, transferring discipline and control to the learners, caring as a means of motivation, the power of discovery, the power of self-evaluation, and facilitating through student encounters. Appropriate loci for facilitating learning include the live-in institution, on-site experiences, and the encounter group.

Bradford, Gibb & Benne (1964) are also concerned with facilitating learning in the encounter group. They present a list of desirable behaviors for group members. These behaviors, symptoms of resolved concerns, are reported in the findings along with the other characteristics of facilitators. A survey of the readings in this book as well as other literature on T-Groups, however, indicates that the formal T-Group depends on an experienced group leader. Non-professionals have caused much harm. The T-Group process, then, is not directly applicable to facilitator groups as they are presently conceived. Furthermore modified T-Group approaches should be carefully developed to avoid dangers alluded to by Bradford et al.

Not only does the facilitator in Ecuador work with groups, some activities concern individuals and are more appropriate to only individuals. Individualization is also an important theme in the literature on helping learners, especially in classrooms. Individualization of instruction is characteristic of competency-based education as well as many forms of non-formal education. Combs (1970) believes educators can help make students more self-directed by (a) believing self-direction is important, (b) trusting in the human organism, (c) maintaining an experimental attitude, and (d) providing opportunities for students (pp. 30-36).

Wilhelms (1970) describes conditions basic to growth in individuality. He mentions stimulation, responsible freedom, support, success, commitment, and self-insight (pp. 37-49). Other more specific conditions which help produce a climate of individuality are listed in a joint statement of National Education Association Departments (Howes, 1970, pp. 183-188). These characteristics have been adapted and reported in the findings of this study on facilitators.

Also related to the area of helping relationships and to the facilitator idea is the aspect of voluntarism. Many facilitators in Ecuador have selected themselves by volunteering. All facilitators are volunteers in the sense that they are not paid for their services.

An analysis of forces supporting individual decisions to volunteer and forces inhibiting individual decisions to volunteer is therefore relevant to the facilitator idea in Ecuador. Schindler-Rainman & Lippitt (1971) provide that analysis (pp. 49-51). A similar analysis of forces affecting the decision to continue, increase commitment, or drop out, is presented (pp. 54-55). Also discussed are the role of orientation, training, follow-up, and inservice training. An ideal training plan for volunteers should include (a) preservice training, (b) start-up support, (c) maintenance-of-effort training, (d) periodic review and feedback, and (e) transition training.

To summarize, the literature on helping relationships provides a variety of perspectives on improving the facilitator concept. Combs' discussion of various kinds of groups and the effective "helper" role in groups sheds new light on the potential of the facilitator. Rogers, Reisser, and Charnofsky are all concerned with how someone "facilitates" learning. Their research also enriches an understanding of the potential of facilitators of NFE. Other contributions are also made by sources dealing with T-Groups, individualization of instruction, and voluntarism.

One problem, however, remains. Throughout the literature on helping relationships unarticulated assumptions are made about leadership. Before proceeding it is necessary to review the basic theories on leadership and a closely related subject, management, in order to put the assumptions into perspective. Although on a more abstract level than some of the practical

concerns raised in this chapter, a deeper understanding of the research on
leadership and management will contribute to an improved facilitator idea.

Leadership and Management

In a doctoral dissertation Bell (1973) reviews the literature on management theory and leadership models. After tracing the development of
management theories from 1900 through 1950, Bell cites Maslow's "hierarchy
of needs" theory as among the most comprehensive and significant theories
between the mid-1940's to the late 1960's.

> Maslow postulated that there were five basic levels of
> human needs: physiological, security, affiliation,
> esteem and self-actualization. Furthermore, these
> need levels tended to arrange themselves along a
> hierarchy in such a way that (1) physiological needs
> must first be satisfied somewhat before security
> needs become dominant, (2) security needs must then
> be satisfied somewhat before affiliation needs become
> dominant, and so forth down the hierarchy (p. 70).

Perhaps the best known of the management theories to emerge in the
1950's, according to Bell (1973), is Douglas McGregor's Theory X-Theory Y.
Theory X assumes that most people are not interested in assuming responsibility and, above all, desire security. Theory Y postulates that people are
not inherently lazy and unreliable, and that they can be basically self-directed
and creative if properly motivated. Therefore, Theory X emphasizes
organizational task orientation while Theory Y emphasizes employee
relationships orientation. Other theorists try to expand the Theory X-

Theory Y continuum or more specifically describe its inner differentiation.

Blanchard and Hersey (1969) explain the difference between management and leadership. Management is defined as "working with and through individuals and groups to accomplish organizational goals (p. 3)." Leadership is "the process of influencing the activities of an individual or group in efforts toward goal achievement in a given situation (p. 60)."

Bell (1973) describes three leadership models which emerged in the mid-1950's. The Ohio State model is based on four quadrants to show the basic combinations of initiating structure and consideration: (a) high consideration and low structure; (b) high structure and high consideration; (c) low structure and low consideration; and (d) high structure and low consideration. Work at the University of Michigan and the group dynamics work of Cartwright and Zander produced the other two models which reinforce the Ohio State model (pp. 80-83).

According to Bell (1973) Blake and Mouton identify five different types of leadership: (a) impoverished--exertion of minimum effort to get required work done; (b) country club--thoughtful attention to needs of people for satisfying relationships; (c) task--efficiency in operations result from arranging conditions of work in such a way that human elements interfere to a minimum degree; (c) middle-of-the-road--balancing the necessity to get out work while maintaining morale of people at a satisfactory level; and

(e) team--interdependence through a "common state" in organization purpose leads to relationships of trust and respect (pp. 83-84).

Hersey (1967) posits a concept of "adaptive leader behavior" which is described as:

> The more a manager adapts his style of leader behavior
> to meet the particular situation and the needs of his
> followers, the more effective he will tend to be in
> reaching personal and organizational goals (p. 15).

Complementing Hersey is Fiedler's "leadership contingency model." Fiedler (1967) feels that the three major situational variables are (a) the leader's personal relations with members of the group; (b) the degree of structure in the task which the group has been assigned to perform; and (c) the power and authority which the leader's position provides.

Finally, Blanchard and Hersey's (1969) "life cycle theory of leadership" suggests that leader behavior should move from high task-low relationships behavior to high task-high relationships behavior to high relationships-low task behavior to low task-low relationships behavior if the followers in the group progress from immaturity to maturity.

Bell (1973) derives five implications from his review of literature on leadership and management: (a) with mature groups there seems to be greater value in developing a learning environment which is participatory, open and honest; (b) since leadership depends on leader behavior, follower behavior, and intervening variables, the more popular notions of leadership as a set of desirable traits, or consistent leadership style are of limited effective-

ness; (c) educational managers need to diagnose accurately the environment

in which leadership and followership are taking place; (d) conflict resolution

may have to occur before any organizational or group leadership can be

effective; and (e) the effectiveness of leader behavior must be related to the

goals of education (pp. 92-96).

Bell (1973) then discusses the emerging roles of competency and

consensus in the Teacher Corps Project which he studied. As a result of that

study, Bell proposes a competency-based leadership model whose essential

dimensions are:

> (a) The maximization of personal power and the minimization
> of position power.
> (b) The operationalization of personal power as conceptual
> competence, volitional competence, technical competence,
> and assessment competence.
> (c) The prevalence of a decision-making environment which
> seeks to resolve conflict by noncoercive means.
> (d) The presence of a high degree of individual and group
> responsibility (p. 249).

The review of leadership and management theory indicates that effective-

ness in these areas is situational. A set of traits may be determined but

they will be of limited effectiveness if followed dogmatically. Decision

making must be shared and noncoercive means must be found to resolve

conflict. The Ecuador Project's facilitator concept is generally consistent

with these conclusions. However the facilitator idea will be strengthened

by a deeper understanding of the evidence on leadership and management
theory.

The Activists

There **is** a final category of literature, relevant to the facilitator idea,
which deals with teacher effectiveness. Often viewed lightly by more
scholarly circles, there is a large body of teachers and writers who base
their approach to educational problems on advocacy, experimentation, action
research, and criticism of schools.

A. S. Neill (1960) is one of the earlier "popular" writers who supports
individualization, elimination of coercion, creativity, and the inclusion of
learners in institutional decision making. Leonard (1968) contributes the
idea of the rogue as teacher and explores the future of education in the "total
environment." He also upholds the parents as educators closely linked with
the formal institutions.

Postman & Weingartner (1969) examine the idea of analyzing information
to determine what is worth knowing. One of the purposes of the book is to
subvert attitudes, beliefs,and assumptions that foster chaos and uselessness.
They also stress the importance of asking relevant, appropriate, and substantial questions. Postman & Weingartner, in considering the characteristics of teachers, **are** interested in what teachers should not do: (a) tell
students what they ought to know; (b) accept a single statement as an answer

to a question; (c) act as a mediator or judge of the quality of ideas expressed; (d) often summarize the positions taken by students on the learning that occurs; and (e) develop lessons from a previously determined "logical" structure (pp. 34-35). They also present a useful technique for facilitating self-expression in learners through poetry (pp. 175-178).

Postman & Weingartner (1971) also present the idea of judo--using the adversary's strength against himself. Examples of how to use judo against traditional schools and teachers are given. Also discussed are counter-productive forms of talk: pomposity, fanaticism (including acceptance of official definitions, rules, and categories, without regard for the realities of particular situations), inanity (ignorance presented under the cloak of sincerity), superstition (ignorance presented under the cloak of authority), earthiness, and sloganeering (pp. 35-39).

In What do I do Monday?, Holt (1970) discusses the teacher as guide. Other sources which take the same approach, and hold some relevance to the facilitator idea are, Thirty-six Children by Herbert Kohl, My Country School Diary by Julia Gordon, and Letter to a Teacher by Schoolboys of Barbiana.

Practical exercises for group dynamics, self-awareness, and opening people up to learning opportunities, are included in Simon's Values Clarification and Shrank's Teaching Human Beings. The exercises tend to be easy and non-threatening. With some adaptation, many would be useful to facilitator learning groups.

Dale's (1972) interest is in building a learning environment. He
presents insightful discussion on three topics useful to those concerned with
facilitating learning: (a) what is worth knowing; (b) learning to learn; and
(c) thinking about thinking. The Center for Curriculum Design (1973) also
deals with environments. This "living-learning catalog" is a directory to non-
school learning--people, places, networks, centers, books, and groups.
Many ideas appear which may be useful to facilitators of community education
activities.

Conclusion

Interestingly the idea of the classroom as a community is strongest
in the activists' writings. A larger number of teachers' skills are expressed
in TABS, various observation instruments, and competency-based education
projects. Useful knowledge and attitudes, as well as other skills, are
suggested by sources dealing with helping relationships and leadership and
management theory. However of all the literature reviewed on teacher
effectiveness the activists provide the most inspiration, if not the most
direction, for improving the facilitator idea.

Recapitulation

In the first chapter some of the dimensions of the crisis in the campo
have been presented. An approach to resolving that crisis, NFE, has been
introduced and defined; and one example of NFE, the University of

Massachusetts' project in Ecuador, has been mentioned. Finally a problem
pertinent to all three subjects has been specified: there is a need to more
fully understand the skills, knowledge, and attitudes of effective facilitators
of NFE in order to improve the facilitator concept and introduce it in other
locations.

Chapter II has examined NFE more fully. Its situational nature has
been discussed and a number of dimensions preferred by the author for
this study, as well as other potential dimensions of NFE have been surveyed.
Finally some problems with the field have been mentioned. From the chapter
a large number of behaviors of effective facilitators of NFE have been
distilled. Those behaviors appear in the Preliminary List of Facilitator
Characteristics (Appendix A).

The third chapter has examined the Ecuador NFE Project in order to
more fully understand the development of the facilitator idea. Evaluation
reports dealing with the Project have also been reviewed for implications
to improve the facilitator idea. Again a considerable number of behaviors
of effective facilitators found in the source have been included in Appendix
B.

Finally the current chapter has looked into the literature on community
development and teacher effectiveness for more suggestions to improve the
existing facilitator idea. The behaviors, stated or implied, which are

relevant to NFE facilitators have been added to the Preliminary List of Characteristics.

The literature which the author considers relevant to this study has been reviewed. A large number of skills, knowledge areas, and attitudes, have been discovered. Now two tasks remain: to determine how experts in the facilitator approach feel about the relevance and importance of those skills, knowledge areas, and attitudes; and to suggest a process whereby selected skills, knowledge, and attitudes can be stated in a form that can be used to help improve the facilitator idea and adapt it to new settings.

CHAPTER IV--FOOTNOTE

[1]A "thana" is an administrative unit of about 100 square miles with more than 200,000 people.

CHAPTER V

THE ORACLES OF QUITO

One aspect of the facilitator idea has not been sufficiently emphasized: there is no single facilitator model. The facilitator idea has been applied in a variety of ways depending on the individual facilitator, the facilitator training, the needs of a particular village, the learners in the evening learning group, and other individuals external to the learning group and often external to the village. Even for two outside observers of the same facilitator and the same conditions the perceptions of the facilitator are likely to vary. So each trainer and each Ecuador Project Staff member carries a slightly (or sometimes greatly) different image of the effective facilitator.

Technical Issues

A technique was needed, then, which would allow each member of the Ecuador staff to pool his or her opinion and contribute toward a group image of the effective facilitator. An assumption made is that each staff member who has observed a facilitator has an insight to contribute to the group opinion. Each member is an oracle--a source of wisdom--concerning the facilitator idea.

The discussion technique was rejected for several reasons. The group could not get together physically without great cost since the Project staff is split between Amherst and Quito. Personalities and social noise tend to distort the dynamics of a face-to-face discussion. Language, including local jargon, is a problem in communication among staff members. A discussion does not insure equal or equitable participation for all involved. A questionnaire seemed more likely to serve the function of discovering individual opinion. But for arriving at a group opinion a one-shot questionnaire is inadequate. The study was immobilized for lack of an instrument or technique for forming a group opinion from the individual members of the Ecuador Project staff. Then the Delphi, a questioning technique consisting of several instruments, was discovered.

The Delphi Technique

Development. Developed by Olaf Helmer and his colleagues at the Rand Corporation in the early 1950's, Delphi was first used to obtain group opinion about urgent defense problems. Named "Delphi" in honor of the oracle of Apollo, the technique is basically a method of collecting and organizing expert opinion on a topic in an effort to produce a convergence of group consensus. This consensus is accomplished through a series of three or four written questionnaires dealing with a variety of questions. Generally, "experts" respond to a set of mailed questionnaires with feedback from each round of questions being used to produce more carefully considered group opinions (Carey, 1972, p. 60).

Characteristics. In his paper entitled, "Predicting the Future," Dalkey explains, "The basic characteristics of the Delphi procedures are: (a) anonymity, (b) iteration with controlled feedback, and (c) statistical group response." Anonymity is achieved by using questionnaires where specific responses are not associated with individual members of the group. In this way the effects of dominant individuals and group pressure are reduced. Iteration consists of performing the interaction among members of the group in several stages. Typically, at the beginning of each stage, group members receive a summary of the results of the previous stage. The members are then asked to reassess their answers considering what the entire group thought on the previous round. Finally, the group opinion is taken as the statistical average of the final opinions of each group member.

Normally the questions to be considered in a Delphi are developed by the investigator. Therefore, the experts' opinions are directed to an established frame of reference. Questions which may be relevant to the study are ignored because they are not included in the first questionnaire. Pfeiffer (1968) mentions a variation of the Delphi which asks the experts to generate the questions to be included in subsequent rounds of the Delphi:

(a) The first questionnaire may call for a list of opinions involving experienced judgment, say a list of predictions or recommended activities.

(b) On the second round each expert receives a copy of the list, and is asked to rate or evaluate each item by such criterion as importance, probability of success, and so on.

(c) The third questionnaire includes the list and the ratings, indicates the consensus if any, and in effect asks the experts either to revise their opinions or else to specify their reasons for remaining outside the concensus.

(d) The fourth questionnaire includes lists of the ratings, the consensus, and minority opinions. It provides a final chance for the revision of opinions (pp. 152-153).

Research by Campbell (1966) and Dalkey (1969) indicate that information gathered using Pfeiffer's approach is more likely to be accurate than that obtained using face-to-face techniques.

Problem areas. A number of limitations to the Delphi Technique have been noted. Basically the limitations are of two types: (a) procedural limitations (those encountered when implementing a Delphi study), and (b) limitations found in Delphi as a forecasting methodology[1] (Waldera, 1971, p. 17).

Procedural problems cited include identifying an "expert" group. Carey (1972) notes that Delphi "is only a tool to help prevent various human factors--such as individual dominance, social noise, and group pressure-- from interferring (p. 62)." Therefore, as Waldera (1971) observes, a Delphi study cannot amount to more than "the sum of the knowledge, opinion, and intuition of the participants involved (p. 20)."

Communicational misunderstandings and time limitation are other

problem areas. Gordon & Amet (1969) are concerned with difficulties which

emerge concerning the lack of precision in wording questions on a question-

naire. This limitation can be lessened, however, "by both participants and

researcher making concerted effort to be as clear and precise as possible

in the wording of questions and of responses (p. 63)." Carey (1972) calls

attention to the time limitation which can influence a Delphi study,

> particularly if feedback responses are not followed
> up in a reasonable amount of time. An extended
> time lag could produce a forgetting of the procedural
> elements, discouragements, and even disinterest on
> the part of the participants. A quick follow-up
> procedure on the part of the researcher could help
> eliminate this problem (p. 63).

A final problem area is creativity. One source observes that the Delphi

technique does not normally promote creative growth of ideas. However,

"By allowing for a set of minority opinions to be expressed by the participants,

this limitation is partially overcome (Carey, 1972, p. 63)."

Applications. The Delphi has been used in a number of educational

research studies which are reviewed by Carey (1972). In addition to fore-

casting and opinion sampling, Delphi has been used to elicit preference

statements from educators or from those with a direct interest in education,

to describe institutional operations in terms of formative evaluation, and to

test the value of Delphi as a forecasting tool.

Cyphert and Gant (1971) present useful generalizations concerning the
Delphi technique which grow out of a study in which they used Delphi:

> (a) prospective participants must be made to feel that
> their response is valid so that they will take part;
> (b) . . . when the feedback was distorted to reflect a
> high ranking, the participants then rated the item
> considerably above average, although it was not
> among the 10 highest ranked targets;
> (c) when respondents disagreed with the consensus
> rating of a goal, they tended to attribute the consensus
> to a group of which they were not a member; and
> (d) virtuallyall (99%) of the respondents' changes in
> opinion occured on Questionnaire III which informed
> them of the first "consensus" reached by the group.
> With hind-sight one can seriously question the need
> for going beyond Questionnaire III (p. 273).

Another study, which was designed to determine the value of Delphi
for forecasting, concludes:

> (a) group opinion coverges after iteration;
> (b) major convergence takes place between round one
> and round two; and
> (c) group response becomes more accurate with
> iteration (Carey, 1972, p. 69).

According to this source controlled anonymous feedback makes the group
estimate more accurate than face-to-face discussion groups (Carey, p. 69).

The Delphi Adapted to the Study of Facilitator Characteristics

Based on the function and advantages of the Delphi, the investigator
decided to use it for this study. For the purpose of this study Pfeiffer's
variation of the Delphi format has been used with one alteration. Due to the

advice of Carey (1972) and Cyphert & Gant (1971) a fourth questionnaire was considered superfluous and was omitted.

The experts. By definition the experts are Ecuador Project staff or former staff who are familiar with nonformal education and who have directly observed facilitators in Ecuador. Since the number of individuals who qualify as experts is quite small, all available potential experts (15) have been included. Of the 15 experts, 13 have participated in all stages of the Delphi. Two potential experts were eliminated from the study. One "lost" his copy of one of the questionnaires; the other returned one of his questionnaires too late to be analyzed. The final group of experts consists of seven Northamericans and six Ecuadorians. There are nine males and four females in the expert group.

Questionnaire I. Each one of the experts received a letter explaining the nature and purpose of the study as well as instructions for completing Questionnaire I which consists of three questions:

> 1. What criteria would you suggest for selecting facilitators to guide educational activities in Ecuadorian communities? What skills, knowledge, attitudes, traits, and other characteristics would you want the facilitator to possess?
> 2. Imagine that you are observing an Ecuadorian facilitator who is extremely effective. What does s/he do to be effective? What skills, knowledge, attitudes, traits and other characteristics does s/he exhibit which makes her/ him effective?
> 3. Imagine that you are observing a very ineffective facilitator. What does s/he do wrong? What skills, knowledge, attitudes, traits and other characteristics does s/he lack?

To insure a high return of completed questionnaires, personal contact was made with each respondent by the investigator or his agent. The questionnaire was translated into Spanish and pilot tested before being sent to the experts.

Preliminary list of characteristics. From the responses to Questionnaire I and the findings in the review of literature, a list of possible skills, knowledge areas, and attitudes of facilitators was compiled. Since the items on the list relate to selection of facilitator trainees or characteristics of facilitators after training, the list of items was divided into those two parts. The items on the two parts of the list were then grouped into categories. Each category is a general skill, knowledge, or attitude area (Appendix A).

Questionnaire II. The general skill, knowledge, or attitude areas became the items for Questionnaire II. Again each expert received a cover letter with instructions for completing Questionnaire II which had two parts corresponding to the two parts of the Preliminary List. Each respondent was asked to rate each item as extremely important, important, preferable but not important ("useful on occasion" replaced "preferable" in part B), or inappropriate. After the items in each section were rated, the respondents were asked to circle five items in part A and ten items in part B which were the "most essential" criteria or characteristics. Respondents were invited to add any items to the list which were missing and to make any comments on any item, observations of unclear items, explanations of answers, or other general or specific comments related to the questionnaire.

Again the questionnaire was translated into Spanish and pilot tested both in Spanish and English. Personal contact with each respondent by the investigator or his agent was again used to insure a high return of the completed questionnaires.

Questionnaire III. This step in the Delphi process consists of basically the same list of items found on Questionnaire II. Six new items, suggested in response to Questionnaire II are included in Questionnaire III. Five items on Questionnaire II were unclear to at least one respondent, so those items were slightly reworded or descriptors were added to clarify the item in question. Each respondent was told how the group had voted on each item in Questionnaire II as well as how he or she had voted. If there existed disagreement between the individual response and the modal group response for any item, the individual was asked to accept the modal group response or state a reason for maintainng a divergent answer. Selected comments made on Questionnaire II were included in Questionnaire III to help each respondent complete Questionnaire III (see Appendix D). This final questionnaire was translated, pilot tested, and delivered to each expert by the investigator or his agent. All thirteen respondents returned the completed questionnaires.

Administrating the Delphi. In order to avoid the general problems

encountered by previous Delphi studies care was taken at each step in the

process. Attention was given to the wording of all items on the questionnaires.

All questionnaires were reviewed by three bilingual persons familiar with

the Ecuador NFE Project. Also a time schedule was followed to prevent

loss of interest and forgetting of procedures by the respondents.

Care was also necessary in order to avoid a problem which was not

encountered by previous Delphi studies: communication between participants

while answering a questionnaire. Since most of the experts worked together

in Amherst or in Quito, the opportunity to discuss answers did arise. To

control this problem the questionnaires were personally delivered by the

investigator in Amherst or by his representative in Quito. Respondents were

requested to work alone by the questionnaire administrators and by instructions

on the questionnaire itself. In only one case involving three respondents

was such communication reported. One of those respondents was not a

member of the final panel of experts. Therefore, this potential problem did

not seriously weaken the study.

Comparison Groups

Since most of the experts' field experience is limited to the Ecuador

Project, the opinions of other individuals is needed for comparison. Criteria

for selecting the other individuals are: (a) extensive experience in some form of out-of-school, community-based education, and (b) little or no knowledge and experience related to Ecuador Project activities. A second and third panel of experts, which met the criteria, were asked to respond to a single questionnaire consisting of the items found on Questionnaire III. The second panel of experts (comparison Group A) is composed of 15 elementary and secondary teachers (about one-half Chicano, one-fourth black, and one-fourth white) all of whom have living and working experience in minority communities. All are enrolled in a course, "Procedures of Investigation and Reporting," at the Institute for Cultural Pluralism at San Diego State University. The third panel of experts (Comparison Group B) is a diverse group which includes 25 extension education workers, former Peace Corps volunteers, community development workers, church workers, social workers, and trainers of community education leaders.

Respondents were asked to rate each item as extremely important, important, preferable but not important ("useful on occasion" on part B), or inappropriate as a criterion or characteristic. The respondents were also asked to circle the five "most essential" criteria on Part A and the ten "most essential" characteristics on part B. They were invited to add any missing items to the list and to make any comments which they felt were appropriate. The results of the two comparison-group questionnaire were compared with the results of the Delphi questionnaire (see Chapter VI).

Operationalization

Since the items expressing facilitator skills, knowledge areas, and attitudes were often vague, abstract, or fragmented, they were operationalized-- stated in terms of directly observable behaviors. A workshop for doctoral students in the Center for International Education was held in which each participant operationalized a selected item (skill, knowledge, or attitude area) according to a specific geographical or cultural setting. In the workshop a workbook was employed which guided participants in the operationalization process (Coffing, Hutchinson, Thomann, & Allan, 1971).

The workbook (Appendix G consists of six steps for operationalizing a goal or intent. By constructing a hypothetical situation participants are asked to observe and record behaviors which indicate the fulfillment of the goal or intent in question. Next participants are asked to record behaviors which prevent the achievement of the goal or intent. The negative behaviors are translated into positive behaviors.

The third step is for participants to form diads, trade lists, and add behaviors to the partner's list. Fourthly, each participant, using his own list, tries to elaborate and more clearly state the positive behaviors listed. The fifth step consists of identifying ideas which have nothing to do with the goal or intent in question. Then the participant is asked to try to relate those irrelevant ideas to the list of positive behaviors in order to add new positive behaviors.

The final step is to examine each item on the list of positive behaviors to see if the item is a directly observable behavior or state. If the item is directly observable it is considered to be operationalized. If the item is not a directly observable behavior or state it is recycled through the six steps.

In the workshops an extra step was inserted into the operationalization process just described. After the third step, each participant was given a copy of the Preliminary List of Facilitator Characteristics. The participant was asked to find the skill, knowledge, or attitude area being operationalized and to examine the specific statements under that area for more ideas to add to the list of positive behaviors. Examples of operationalized items can be found in Chapter VI.

Ethical Issues

Most studies are not concerned with ethical issues in the procedure of the research. However this study of facilitators in Ecuador involves cross-cultural collection and analysis of data. Experience has shown that some important issues must be considered in this type of study. Perhaps the best example of the cause for ethical concerns in research design is Project Camelot.

Project Camelot

In 1964, "the largest single grant ever provided for a social science project," brought this Project into being. The objective of Project Camelot was:

> to determine the feasibility of developing a general
> social systems model which would make it possible
> to predict and influence politically significant aspects
> of social change in the developing nations of the
> world (Horowitz, pp. 4 & 5).

The scientific limits of Project Camelot were never stated. That the study

was supported by the United States Army and Department of Defense was

stated but was not widely known.

Dr. Johan Galtung, who was in Chile and was associated with the Latin

American Faculty of Social Science, was invited to participate in Project

Camelot. He declined for several reasons: (a) he could not accept the role

of the Army as a sponsoring agent interested in a study of counterinsurgency;

(b) he saw the Army as an agency for managing conflict, even promoting

conflict, not as an agency of development; (c) he noted several "imperialistic

features" of the research design; and (d) he found the study to be "asymmetrical"

in that it would provide information to the Army on counter-insurgency in

Latin America but would not study the conditions under which Latin American

nations might intervene in the affairs of the United States. Dr. Galtung shared

documents describing the purpose and sponsorship of Project Camelot,

documents which Project Camelot had sent to a restricted list of social

scientists, with colleagues throughout Latin America (Horowitz, 1967, pp.

12-13).

When a social scientist associated with Project Camelot solicited the
cooperation of the Vice-Chancellor of the University of Chile, misrepresenting
himself and the nature of the study, he was confronted by the restricted
documents which Dr. Galtung had freely circulated.   Project Camelot was
then denounced by the University of Chile and the Chilean mass communications
network causing the United States Ambassador to request an unconditional
cancellation of Project Camelot's Chilean activities.   Following hearings before
the House Foreign Affairs Committee in Washington, Project Camelot was
cancelled by the Defense Department.   The study was terminated less than a
year after it began (Horowitz, 1967, pp. 11-16).

Asymmetic Research

In a book describing Project Camelot and its aftermath, Galtung raises
the issue of "scientific colonialism" of which Project Camelot was an example.
"By scientific colonialism we shall refer to a process whereby the center of
gravity for the acquisition of knowledge about the nation is located outside the
nation itself (Horowitz, 1967, p. 296)." Aspects of scientific colonialism, or
asymmetric research, include biased distribution or accumulation of
personally acquired knowledge about the "colony," covert administration of
data collection and analysis, classifying results of the study, and not fully
informing those who are studied about the design, purpose, sponsorship, or
instrumentation of the study.

Galtung suggests the following remedies to asymmetric research:
(a) frankness where purpose and sponsorship are concerned; (b) require
that social science projects be unclassified; (c) see that the tools of social
science are more equally distributed; (d) make sure local personnel have
access to the results of the research; (e) third parties or international
institutes should conduct research of a politically touchy nature; and (f) there
should be more openness about the entire problem. He also presents a
"recipe for symmetric organization" of a research project initiated by social
scientists in a developed country to study conditions in a developing country:
participation of scholars from the country studied in the research design,
data collection at all levels, data processing at all levels, theory formation,
and write-up. Galtung also emphasizes that the scholars from the developing
country should have equal access to raw data. He recognizes, however,
"these conditions will have to be tempered by local circumstances. . ."

An Ethical Procedure for Investigating Facilitators

Since this study includes an attempt by a scholar in the United States to
describe an aspect of a project based in Ecuador, Galtung's guidelines are
relevant. An attempt has been made to follow those guidelines through the
following actions: (a) the purpose and sponsorship of the study were made
clear in the first cover letter sent to all participants in the study; (b) the study
is not classified in any way; (c) the tools and procedures used in the study are

simple enough that the descriptions and examples included in the study are sufficient so that any researcher in any country may understand and adapt any of those tools or procedures; (d) the results of the study has been made available to anyone requesting it; and (e) an Ecuadorian and former director of the Ecuador Project was invited to participate in all stages of the development, administration, and analysis of the study as an ex officio member of the investigator's academic advisory committee.

Summary

The data-gathering technique used for this study is a three-part Delphi questionnaire. Questionnaire I asked the selected group of 13 experts to brainstorm characteristics of effective facilitators. Questionnaire II incorporated the responses to Questionnaire I and the review of literature into a list of two parts: criteria for selecting facilitator trainees and characteristics of effective facilitators after training. The experts were asked to rate the importance of each criterion or characteristic. Questionnaire III consists of the same items as Questionnaire II but provides feedback on group and individual ratings from Questionnaire II. The experts were asked to reassess their answers in light of the feedback.

The final list of items was also sent to two comparison groups for their ratings. The comparison group questionnaires are single questionnaires, not Delphis. Finally selected items on the list of facilitator characteristics were operationalized--submitted to a process to produce directly observable behaviors.

In the procedure just described the Oracles of Quito--Ecuador Project staff members who have worked in Ecuador and who have observed facilitators--contributed their individual opinions to a group opinion. This group opinion of the importance of facilitator characteristics is important for improving the facilitator in Ecuador and for adapting the facilitator idea to other potential settings where it is appropriate.

CHAPTER V--FOOTNOTE

[1]Since the Delphi is not used for forecasting in this study of facilitator characteristics, those limitations may be overlooked.

CHAPTER VI

CHARACTERISTICS OF FACILITATORS

This chapter, which presents the findings of the study, begins with a brief discussion of the Preliminary List of Facilitator Characteristics. The List, which comes from the review of literature and Questionnaire I, is the source of items for subsequent questionnaires. The results of each of those questionnaires is then analyzed. The responses to Questionnaires II and III are also compared. Apart from the Delphi questionnaires, the results of a one-shot questionnaire given to two comparison groups are also analyzed for each group. Then the results of all four questionnaires which deal with specific facilitator characteristics are compared. Finally operationalized statements for selected facilitator characteristics are presented.

Preliminary List of Characteristics

The review of literature and the administration of Questionnaire I yield a large number of explicit and implicit statements concerning the skills, knowledge, and attitudes of facilitators of NFE. Those statements are organized thematically into more general skill, knowledge, and attitude "areas." Overlapping statements are combined and most of the items are reworded for the purpose of uniformity of expression. Still, the statements represent a wide diversity of specificity ranging from vague assumptions to quite specific behaviors. The statements are divided into criteria for selection and characteristics of facilitators after training (see Appendix A).

The classification and organization of the items was a difficult and tedius task. In many cases the classification may seem arbitrary. Certain general skill, knowledge, and attitude areas overlap, and may be combined. Other general areas may be divided. The organization and classification of the list, however, depends on the manner in which the list is used and the particular setting for which it is used. The current list represents the author's classification and organization according to the needs of the study. The list is based on his understanding of Ecuadorian villages where the facilitator idea is being implemented.

Most of the sources listed in the bibliography have been used to compile this list. However some sources are more fertile than others. Especially helpful are Paulston (1973a), Hoxeng (1973), Ickis (1972), Swanson (1973), Batten (1959, 1965), Nylen et al. (1967), Clinic to Improve (1973), Schmuck & Schmuck (1971), Forman (E. P. D. , 1974), and Smith et al (E. P. D. , 1974). The list is called a preliminary list because many of the specific items are vague and difficult to interpret. The list will remain a "preliminary" list until it is operationalized, translated into behavioral statements for facilitators in a particular situation.

177

Questionnaire II

The general skill areas from the Preliminary List of Characteristics became the base for Questionnaire II. In the first part of the questionnaire, a separate item, "has considerably schooling," was added. Although this item is directly opposed to the rhetoric of the Ecuador Project staff and to NFE as it has been defined, the item was added to keep the list from seeming to present an "ideal facilitator model." The item dealing with "proven leader" was written as two items: "proven leader (formal elected or appointed position)" and "proven leader (informal activities)." Likewise "selected by the community" was included in the questionnaire as two options: "selected by the community democratically" and "selected by the community using the method normally used to make decisions in that community." The two options represent two sides of a debate within the Ecuador Project staff. The options were added to clarify some of the issues in that debate and to see if the experts generally favor one of the options.

In the second part of the questionnaire "non-verbal communication skills," which was originally considered to be part of discussion skill, is presented as a separate item. "Helps professional teachers improve schools" was added to the list. Again this item is in conflict with Ecuador Project rhetoric and activities but it was added to keep the list from seeming to express an ideal model.

178

An analysis of the response to questionnaire indicates that the experts consider virtually all of the items relevant skills, knowledge, and attitudes, of effective facilitators. At least one expert rates the item "inappropriate" in thirteen of the twenty-two items in part A and in ten of the thirty-nine items in part B. However only one item is considered inappropriate by half the experts (for the items rated "inappropriate," the average number of experts who gave that rating is 1.8). Therefore the "inappropriate" ratings generally represent isolated individual opinions. Six experts rate "has considerable schooling" as "inappropriate;" the other six rate the item as "preferable but not important" (one did not rate the item). This item is also the only item which indicates any apparent polarization between Ecuadorians and North Americans on the Project Staff. Four Ecuadorians and two North Americans rate the item as "preferable" while five North Americans and one Ecuadorian rate it as "inappropriate." The other item which was anticipated to be rejected, "helps professional teachers improve schools," is rated as "preferable" by nine of twelve experts who voted.

Other responses are closer to those anticipated. Informal leadership is definitely favored over formal leadership and a democratic community selection process is favored over "the method normally used to make decisions in that community." However, in the latter case the preference is not overwhelming.

In order to compare the relative importance of items according to the experts, the votes have been given a numerical value: inappropriate = -1; preferable or useful on occasion = 1; important = 2; extremely important = 3. Those items which were indicated as "most essential" received another point. The votes have been totaled and the items have been ranked. Since virtually all of the items are considered relevant (extremely important, important, or preferable) the rank order represents extremely small differences between items (e.g., the difference between the tenth and fourteenth ranked items is only three points). The rank order for part A is:

1. Dynamic and open;
2. Flexible and creative;
3. Respected and accepted by a wide variety of community members;
4. Understands the nature of potential work in the community;
5. Stable personal and family situation;
6. Believes people should constantly aspire to improve themselves and their communities;
7. Experience in civic and community affairs;
8. Proven leader (informal activities);
8. Life style does not conflict with the community;
10. Available;
10. Selected by the community democratically;
12. Basic ability in reading, writing and math;
13. Independent yet cooperative;
14. Likeable;
15. Organized and dependable;
16. Keeps up with the local, regional, and national news;
16. Sensitive, considerate, and open to people from different backgrounds;
18. Possesses strong beliefs in the potential of NFE;
19. Selected by the community using the method normally used to make decisions in that community;
20. Proven leader (formal elected or appointed position);
21. Has considerable schooling.

The rank order for part B is:

1. Discussion/Dialogue skills;
2. Able to effect horizontal relationships;
3. Able to increase peoples self-confidence;
4. Group dynamics skills;
4. Skill in aiding community planning;
6. Able to bring people together;
7. Skill in dealing with diverse individual needs and abilities;
7. Able to catalyze cooperation among people;
7. Able to discover and articulate the learning needs present in the community;
7. Negotiation skills;
11. Sensitive to the feelings, attitudes, and relationships of people;
12. Sees development as a process of liberation from domination and dependence;
12. Able to catalyze community projects;
14. Analytical and evaluation skills;
14. Ability to motivate;
14. Skill in building community support;
14. Believes people should constantly aspire to improve themselves and their environment;
18. Able to stimulate community organization;
18. Confronts resistance to individual or community development;
20. Problem-solving activity skills;
20. Training skills;
20. Aware of what other individuals, groups, and communities have done to improve themselves;
23. Able to develop a communication network;
23. Skill in working with community leaders;
23. Able to broaden access to information;
26. Speaking skill;
27. Questioning skill;
27. Skill in pacing;
27. Able to simultaneously pursue multiple goals;
27. Functional literacy and numeracy skills;
31. Non-verbal communication skills;
32. Ability to match learning needs to learning resources and opportunities;
32. Skill in a variety of learning techniques;
34. Knows NFE from formal education;

35. Skill in planning NFE activities;
36. Able to stimulate planning on the family level;
37. Knowledge of content areas pertinent to development;
38. Materials development skills;
39. Helps professional teachers improve schools.

Six new items were suggested in response to Questionnaire II. In part A "possesses a strong sense of cultural pride" was added. In part B the following items were suggested by the experts: "believes in the possibility of change, in people's capacity to grow and in people's potential; believes in the strength of shared decision-making; delegates authority; shows confidence in own skills as a leader; motivated to continue beyond scope of immediate support." Although each of these items is implied in other items already on the list, the suggested items were included in Questionnaire III as separate items.

Questionnaire III

With the addition of the new items, Questionnaire II became Questionnaire III. Five items were reworded slightly to improve clarity due to comments on responses to Questionnaire II. With information on the response to Questionnaire II, the experts rated the items again on Questionnaire III.

The only item rated "inappropriate" is "has considerable schooling" (the same as with questionnaire II). Only 18 items received a vote of "inappropriate" and the average number of experts who voted each of those 18 items "inappropriate" is 1.7.

Using the same mathematical weighting of votes as in the analysis of

Questionnaire II, the responses to Questionnaire III yield the following rank

order for part A:

1. Possesses a strong sense of cultural pride;
2. Flexible and creative;
3. Dynamic and open;
4. Available;
4. Life style does not conflict with the community;
6. Believes people should constantly aspire to improve themselves and their community;
7. Understands the nature of potential work in the community;
8. Proven leader (informal activities);
8. Experience in civic and community affairs;
10. Stable personal and family situation;
10. Basic ability in reading, writing and math;
10. Selected by the community democratically;
13. Respected and accepted by a wide variety of community members;
14. Keeps up with the local, regional, and national news;
15. Organized and dependable;
15. Likeable;
17. Independent yet cooperative;
17. Selected by the community using the method normally used to make decisions in the community;
19. Sensitive, considerate, and open to people from different backgrounds;
20. Possesses strong beliefs in the potential of NFE;
21. Proven leader (formal elected or appointed position); and
22. Has considerable schooling.

The rank order for part B is:

1. Discussion/Dialogue skills;
1. Able to increase people's confidence;
1. Skill in aiding community planning;
4. Able to bring people together;
4. Sensitive to the feelings, attitudes and relationships of people;
4. Believes in the strength of shared decision-making;

7. Able to effect horizontal relationships;
7. Skill in dealing with diverse individual needs and abilities;
7. Negotiation skills;
11. Group dynamics skills;
11. Analytical and evaluation skills;
13. Sees development as a process of liberation from domination and dependence;
14. Believes in the possibility of change, in people's capacity to grow and in people's potential;
14. Able to discover and articulate the learning needs present in the community;
16. Delegates authority;
17. Ability to motivate;
17. Motivated to continue beyond scope of immediate support;
19. Questioning skill;
20. Problem-solving skill;
20. Able to stimulate community organization;
20. Training skills;
23. Speaking skill;
23. Skill in building community support;
23. Skill in working with community leaders;
26. Able to broaden access to information;
26. Able to catalyze community projects;
26. Able to develop a communications network;
26. Confronts resistance to individual or community development;
26. Aware of what other individuals, groups, and communities have done to improve themselves;
26. Shows confidence in own skills as a leader;
32. Non-verbal communication skills;
33. Skill in a variety of learning techniques;
33. Ability to match learning needs to learning resources and opportunities;
33. Functional literacy and numeracy skills;
33. Believes people should constantly aspire to improve themselves and their environment;
37. Knows NFE from formal education;
38. Skill in pacing;
39. Able to simultaneously pursue multiple goals;
40. Able to stimulate planning on the family level;
41. Skill in planning NFE/Facilitator activities;
42. Knowledgeable of content areas pertinent to development;
42. Materials development skills;

44. Helps professional teachers improve schools.

Since the rank order of items based on the response to Questionnaire III is the final and most important indication of the relative importance of items, it is interesting to note the absolute importance according to the experts. In part A a majority of experts agree that the items ranked 1 through 7 are all extremely important. Items 8 through 19 on the rank order lists are important; items 20 and 21 are preferable but not important; and item 11 is inappropriate according to a majority of the experts. There are two exceptions to this analysis: items ranked 10 and 17 pertaining to selection by the community indicate no clear preference by the experts. According to the numerical weighting, a "democratic" process is preferred over the "normal decision-making method." However, more experts indicate that the latter is extremely important than rate the former extremely important. For both items the voting is spread over the possible responses. No majority consensus is achieved.

In part B a majority of the experts feel that items 1 through 17 (ability to motivate) on the rank order list are extremely important. Items 17 (motivated to continue beyond scope of immediate support) through 38 are important and items 39 through 44 are useful on occasion. No item on part B is inappropriate according to the experts. The one exception to this analysis is the item ranked 41, "skill in planning NFE/Facilitator activities." A majority of experts feel that the item is important rather than useful on occasion.

Again the only apparent polarization between Ecuadorians and North-americans is on the item, "has considerable schooling." Five North-americans and two Ecuadorians call it "inappropriate" while four Ecuadorians and two Northamericans call it "preferable." A majority of Ecuadorians feel this criteria is relevant while a majority of Northamericans feel it is inappropriate. The responses were also analyzed comparing ethnic back-grounds (Quechua compared to non-Quechua), Northamerican academic back-ground with Quechua background, and Northamerican academic background with Ecuadorian field experience. Generally there is striking agreement between groups in each comparison.

Although virtually no polarization is evident there are differences between groups. Most of those differences concern agreement within one group as opposed to agreement within another group. Six of the seven Northamericans rate the seventh ranked item on part A (understands the nature of potential work in the community) as extremely important and the fifteenth ranked item (organized and dependable) as important. On part B six of the seven North-americans rate the forty-first item (skill in planning NFE/Facilitator activities) as important and all seven rate the forty-second ranked item (materials development skills) as preferable. While the modal response of the Ecuadorians agrees with the Northamericans in each case, the Ecuadorians' responses are widely distributed over the possible responses.

The Ecuadorians agree unanimously that the item ranked tenth on part A (basic ability in reading, writing, and math) is important and that the item ranked thirty-ninth on part B (able to simultaneously pursue multiple goals) is preferable but not important. The modal response of the Northamericans in each case agrees with the Ecuadorians but the Northamericans' responses vary widely over the possible ratings.

In comparing the three Quechua experts with the rest of the group, the former agree on the ratings of three items while the other ten experts are in wide disagreement. According to the Quechua experts item 17 on part A (selected by the community using the method normally used to make decisions in the community) is extremely important; item 19 (sensitive, considerate, and open to people from different backgrounds, is important; and item 39 (able to simultaneously pursue multiple goals) is preferable but not important.

There is polarization between the four academic Northamericans in one group and the three experts of Quechua background in the other group on one item. The tenth ranked item on part A (selected by the community democratically) is rated preferable by three Northamericans and important by the other. Two Quechua staff members rate the item extremely important. On item 19 (sensitive, open, and considerate to people from different backgrounds) all of the Quechua group vote for an "important" rating while the four Northamericans are perfectly disagreed.

In comparing the four Northamerican academics with the four Ecuadorians with the most field experience there is polarization again on the tenth ranked item on part A (selected by the community democratically). Three Northamericans vote for preferable and one votes for important. Three Ecuadorians vote for extremely important and one votes for important. The Northamericans strongly agree that items 7 (understands the nature of potential work in the community) and 17 (independent yet cooperative) on part A are extremely important and important respectively. On part B the North-americans strongly agree that item 41 (skill in planning NFE/Facilitator activities is important and that item 42 (materials development skills) is preferable but not important. On each of the last four items the Ecuadorians with field experience disagree within their group.

Such differences in opinion within groups may be quite important. Although the modal concensus is clear the suggestion of agreement may be misleading when there is a wide range in the responses. It is difficult, however to draw strong conclusions based on this analysis since the groups are quite small when the thirteen experts are divided for comparison. An additional weakness in the analysis is the division of the experts into groups. The only easy (and meaningful) division is Northamericans versus Ecuadorians. Other divisions are more subjective. These divisions were made after direct consultation with the experts but the divisions are still somewhat controversial.

Attempts were also made to analyze the responses to Questionnaire III by dividing the experts into other groups. These attempts yield no answer to the basic question asked in the analysis of the questionnaires, "What factors account for the rating and ranking of items?"

Questionnaire III was also analyzed in terms of the concreteness or abstractness of items in order to account for differences in rating or ranking of items. Generally speaking higher rankings might be expected of more abstract items and lower ratings might be expected of concrete items. Three individuals were asked to rate each item as abstract (general, hard to define, comprehensive, inclusive, hard to observe with precision), concrete (specific, exclusive, easy to define, particular, easy to observe), or somewhere in between. An average of the three individuals' responses for each item was compared with the rankings for Questionnaire III items. Based on the analysis there is no pattern in the relationship between an item's ranking and its degree of abstractness. Items which are high on the list have high, low, and median degrees of abstractness. Likewise items which are ranked low are considered abstract, concrete, and in between.

The analysis of the abstractness of items does raise other questions. Ratings varied widely among the three individuals (two have extensive experience with the Ecuador Project, one has little experience with it) indicating that for most of the questions abstractness is a very subjective rating depending on personal variables more than variables external to the

individual raters. A second and related question raised is that degree of
abstractness may be inversely proportional to degree of familiarity with an
item. Based on the data and the analysis those two questions cannot be
answered.

In general an analysis of responses to Questionnaire III by nationality,
ethnic characteristics, field experience or academic background of respondents is unable to explain differences in ratings or rankings of items. Likewise degree of abstractness appears to be unrelated to the ratings or rankings.
The overwhelming impression from analysis of responses is that the importance
of the items accounts for their rating and that there is strong agreement
among the experts on the ratings.

Comparison of Questionnaire II and Questionnaire III

According to the literature on the Delphi technique the group should
tend toward consensus in successive rounds and the group opinion should
become increasingly accurate. Consensus definitely became clearer in
Questionnaire III. On Questionnaire II at least one-half of the experts agreed
on their responses to 36 out of 61 items. This means that consensus of at
least half of the experts was achieved on 59% of the items. On Questionnaire
III 98% of the items showed a consensus of at least one-half of the experts
(the only exception is "selected by the community democratically"). There
was agreement of at least 9 of the 13 experts on 92% of the items in Questionnaire III.

Apparently, the experts' opinions became stronger as they responded to Questionnaire II and Questionnaire III. The number of abstentions was greatly decreased in Questionnaire III as compared to Questionnaire II.

In general the rank order of items established in Questionnaire II is confirmed by the rank order in Questionnaire III. Those changes which did occur can be attributed to one or more of the following: (a) the introduction of new items; (b) the rewording of some items for clarity; (c) the elimination of the "most essential" rating of items in Questionnaire III; as well as (d) changes of opinion by the experts.

In summary the emerging trends in responses which are manifested in Questionnaire II become clearer in Questionnaire III. With the exceptions noted, Questionnaire III indicates a clear group opinion on the items. If the literature and research on the Delphi as a research instrument are correct, the responses to Questionnaire III are more accurate than the responses to Questionnaire II.

Comparison Groups

Since the experts have one striking commonality in their backgrounds (all have worked on the Ecuador Project) a comparison group was needed to check the experts' opinion. Questionnaire III was sent to two groups of respondents. Members of both groups were selected on the basis of strong experience in some form of "out-of-school" education. A second criterion was that no respondent should be familiar with the Ecuador NFE Project.

The first group consists of seventeen teachers in minority communities near San Diego, California. All have living and working experience in the minority communities. Approximately one-half of the respondents are Chicanos, one-fourth are Black, and one-fourth are White.

The second group is diverse. Questionnaires were mailed to thirty-eight individuals who met the criteria for respondents. Twenty-five replied including extension workers at state, district, and county levels, people with international community development experience in various countries, social and community development workers in U.S. minority communities, educators associated with NFE programs, two ministers active in community education, and one specialist in adult basic education. Some of the respondents are citizens of other countries, some are university students or faculty members, and some are employed in out-of-school educational programs.

Neither of the two comparison groups represents a random sample. Although an effort was made to secure wide diversity in participation, the respondents are not intended to be representative of all or even most groups which meet the criteria for respondents. The respondents only represent a point of view not formed or influenced by association with the Ecuador NFE Project.

Comparison group A questionnaire. As with the Ecuador Project
experts, this group considers vitually all of the items relevant skills,
knowledge, or attitudes, of effective facilitators. The single exception is
"proven leader (formal elected or appointed position)" where 12 respondents
rate the item "inappropriate and 5 respondents call it "preferable." Twenty-
eight items receive an "inappropriate" rating from at least one expert; however
the mean average of inappropriate votes is only two and one-half of the
seventeen experts.

With respect to the options included in the questionnaire, informal
leadership is preferred over formal leadership as a selection criterion;
and the "method normally used to make decisions in the community" is
favored (very narrowly) over a democratic facilitator selection process
in the community.

Again the votes were mathematically weighted and totaled for each item
to yield a rank order of items. According to the respondents the order of
importance of the items for part A is:

1. Sensitive, considerate, and open to people from
   different backgrounds;
2. Flexible and creative;
3. Possesses a strong sense of cultural pride;
4. Understands the nature of potential work in the community;
5. Organized and dependable;
6. Life style does not conflict with the community;
7. Available;
8. Basic ability in reading; writing, and math;

9. Possesses strong beliefs in the potential of out-of-school education;
10. Likeable;
11. Dynamic and open;
11. Respected and accepted by a wide variety of community members;
13. Experience in civic and community affairs;
14. Believes people should constantly aspire to improve themselves and their communities;
15. Keeps up with the local, regional, and national news;
16. Independent yet cooperative;
17. Stable personal and family situation;
18. Proven leader (informal activities);
19. Selected by the community using the method normally used to make decisions in that community;
20. Has considerable schooling;
21. Selected by the community democratically; and
22. Proven leader (formal elected or appointed position).

The rank order for part B is:

1. Believe in the possibility of change, in people's capacity to grow and in people's potential;
2. Sensitive to the feelings, attitudes, and relationships of people;
3. Ability to motivate;
4. Able to discover and articulate the learning needs present in the community;
5. Skill in dealing with diverse individual needs and abilities;
6. Discussion/Dialogue skills;
7. Group dynamics skills;
8. Able to bring people together;
9. Able to increase people's self-confidence;
10. Believes in the strength of shared decision-making;
11. Able to catalyze community projects;
12. Training skills;
12. Ability to match learning needs to learning resources and opportunities;
12. Skill in working with community leaders;
12. Skill in building community support;
12. Able to broaden access to information;

17. Analytical and evaluation skills;
17. Knowledgeable of content areas pertinent to development;
17. Shows confidence in own skills as a leader;
20. Skill in aiding community planning;
21. Motivated to continue beyond the scope of immediate support;
21. Problem-solving activity skills;
23. Able to catalyze cooperation among people;
23. Sees development as a process of liberation from domination and dependence;
25. Able to develop a communication network;
25. Skill in pacing;
25. Non-verbal communication skills;
28. Speaking skill;
28. Able to stimulate community organization;
31. Skill in planning facilitator activities;
32. Skill in a variety of learning techniques.
33. Confronts resistance to individual or community development;
34. Delegates authority;
34. Negotiation skills;
36. Knows formal from out-of-school education;
36. Materials development skills;
38. Aware of what other individuals, groups, and communities have done to improve themselves;
39. Helps professional teachers improve schools;
39. Able to simultaneously pursue multiple goals;
41. Functional literacy and numeracy skills;
41. Believes people should constantly aspire to improve themselves and their environment;
41. Able to effect horizontal relationships; and
44. Able to stimulate planning on the family level.

Compared to Questionnaires II and III there is less agreement as to the absolute rating of items. At least half of the respondents agreed to the rating of 56% of the items (compared with 59% on Questionnaire II and 98% on Questionnaire III).

Comparison group B questionnaire. According to this group of respondents all of the items are relevant. No more than six of the twenty-five respondents rated any item "inappropriate." Thirty-three items received an "inappropriate" rating from at least one expert; but the mean average of experts rating those thirty-three items "inappropriate" is two.

Group opinion on this questionnaire clearly favors informal leadership experience over formal appointed or elected leadership experience as a selection criterion. The group ranks the "normal method of making decisions" above a democratic process of selecting facilitators by the community.

In order to rank the items by their relative importance according to the respondents, the votes were totaled in the same manner as for the previous questionnaires. The items in order of relative importance for part A are:

1. Available;
2. Respected and accepted by a wide variety of community members;
3. Sensitive, considerate and open to people from different backgrounds;
3. Flexible and creative;
5. Possesses strong beliefs in the potential of out-of-school education;
6. Understands the nature of potential work in the community;.
7. Stable personal and family situation;
8. Organized and dependable;
9. Possesses a strong sense of cultural pride;

10. Believes people should constantly aspire to improve themselves and their communities;
11. Life style does not conflict with the community;
12. Proven leader (informal activities);
12. Basic ability in reading, writing, and math;
14. Experience in civic and community affairs;
15. Selected by the community using the method normally used to make decisions in that community;
15. Likeable;
17. Dynamic and open;
18. Independent yet cooperative;
19. Keeps up with the local, regional, and national news;
20. Has considerable schooling;
21. Selected by the community democratically; and
22. Proven leader (formal elected or appointed position).

The ranking of items in part B is:

1. Believes in the possibility of change, in people's capacity to grow, and in people's potential;
2. Ability to match learning needs to learning resources;
3. Able to discover and articulate learning needs present in the community;
3. Able to increase people's self-confidence;
3. Ability to motivate;
6. Discussion/dialogue skills;
7. Skill in working with community leaders;
7. Sensitive to the feelings, attitudes, and relationships of people;
9. Skill in building community support;
9. Able to catalyze cooperation among people;
11. Able to catalyze community projects;
11. Skill in planning facilitator activities;
13. Able to broaden access to information;
13. Skill in dealing with diverse individual needs and abilities;
13. Problem-solving activity skills;
16. Believes in the strength of shared decision making;
17. Non-verbal communication skills;
17. Analytical and evaluation skills;
19. Motivated to continue beyond scope of immediate support;
19. Training skills;

19. Able to stimulate community organization;
22. Able to bring people together;
23. Skill in aiding community planning;
24. Shows confidence in own skills as a leader;
24. Knowledgeable of content areas pertinent to development;
26. Able to effect horizontal relationships;
26. Group dynamics skills;
28. Speaking skill;
28. Believes people should constantly aspire to improve themselves and their environment;
30. Able to simultaneously pursue multiple goals;
30. Skill in pacing;
32. Questioning skill;
33. Negotiation skills;
33. Delegates authority;
35. Skill in a variety of learning techniques;
36. Able to develop a communication network;
37. Aware of what other individuals, groups, and communities have done to improve themselves;
38. Functional literacy and numeracy skills;
39. Helps professional teachers improve schools;
40. Knows formal from out-of-school education;
41. Sees development as a process of liberation from domination and dependence;
42. Confronts resistance to individual and community development;
42. Materials development skills; and
44. Able to stimulate planning on a family level.

In terms of group agreement on the rating of each item, at least one-half of the respondents agree on 56% of the items. This degree of agreement is identical to the other comparison group response.

Comparison of Questionnaires

Since virtually all of the items on all four questionnaires (excluding Questionnaire I which did not deal with particular items) are relevant according to the respondents, the only differences are in degree of importance. Of the ratings, then "extremely important" is the most interesting. Tables I and II list the items which were rated "extremely important" on Questionnaire III. The rank and rating of each of these items is compared for all four questionnaires.

Generally the comparison groups confirm the importance of the seven items in ·part A. "Dynamic and open" is ranked considerably lower by both comparison groups. The only other major difference is in rating: Comparison Group B agrees that two items (life style does not conflict with the community; and understands the nature of potential work in the community) are important as opposed to the "extremely important" rating given by respondents to Questionnaire III.

In part B the most striking difference is on the ability to effect horizontal relationships. Both comparison groups rank this skill well below the ranking by the Ecuador Project staff. It is ranked forty-first on the list of 44 items on part B by Comparison Group A. Other items which the comparison groups rank considerably lower than the Ecuador Project staff does are: skill in aiding community planning; negotiation skills; seeing development as a process of liberation from domination and dependence; and delegating authority.

TABLE I

Comparison of Questionnaires for Part A--
Criteria for Selecting Facilitator Trainees

Items Questionnaire*	RANKING				RATING			
	Q-II	Q-III	CG-A	CG-B	Q-II	Q-III	CG-A	CG-B
Selection criteria								
Possesses a strong sense of cultural pride	**	1	3	9	**	E	E	
Flexible and creative	2	2	2	3		E	E	E
Dynamic and open	1	3	11	17	E	E		
Available	10	4	6	1		E	E	E
Life style does not conflict with the community	8	4	6	11		E		I
Believes people should aspire to improve themselves	6	6	14	10		E		
Understands the nature of potential work in community	4	7	4	6	E	E	E	I

* Q-Questionnaire
 CG-Comparison Group
** item was introduced <u>after</u> this questionnaire.
***E - extremely important
 I - important
 BLANK - no agreement by at least one half of the respondents.

TABLE II

Comparison of Questionnaires for Part B--
Characteristics of Effective Facilitators After Training

Items Questionnaire*	RANKING				RATING			
	Q-II	Q-III	CG-A	CG-B	Q-II	Q-III	CG-A	CG-B
Facilitator characteristics after training								
Discussion/dialogue skills	1	1	6	6	E	E	E	E
Able to increase people's confidence	2	1	8	3	E	E	E	E
Skill in aiding community planning	4	1	20	23	E	E	I	
Able to bring people together	6	4	8	22	E	E	E	I
Sensitive to feelings, attitudes, relationships of people	11	4	2	7	E	E	E	E
Believes in the strength of shared decision making	**	4	10	16	**	E	E	E
Able to effect horizontal relationships	2	7	41	26	E	E		
Skill in dealing with diverse individual needs and abilities	7	7	5	13	E	E	E	I
Able to catalyze cooperation among people	7	7	23	9	E	E		
Negotiation skills	7	7	34	33	E	E		I
Group dynamics skills	4	11	7	26	E	E	E	E
Analytical & evaluation skills	14	11	17	17	E	E	E	
Sees development as a process of liberation from domination and dependence	12	13	23	41	E	E		
Believes in the possibility of change and in people's potential	**	14	1	1	**	E	E	E
Able to discover and articulate learning needs present in the community	7	14	4	3		E	E	E
Delegates authority	**	16	34	33	**	E		I
Ability to motivate	14	17	3	3		E	E	E

Considered together the differences in ranking seem to point out a discrepancy in perspective between the Project staff and others. The Project staff seem to view development as a process that occurs from within the community and leadership as a role among peers. On the other hand the comparison groups seem to view development in terms of outside intervention in the communities and leadership in terms of vertical relationships. Those items which indicate a consolidation of authority and reasponsibility by the facilitator are rated higher than those items which indicate a transfer of authority and responsibility to the community. The comparison groups seem to see the facilitator as a person who organizes and acts. The Ecuador Project staff seem to see the facilitator as a person who helps others to organize and to act for themselves.

Clearly, in applying the findings of this study, different groups will have different perceptions and different uses for the facilitator idea. Each group or individual who tries to adapt the facilitator characteristics to a particular setting will likely rank the items differently. Items high on the list will probably be carefully considered. Items low on the list will probably be ignored altogether.

Adapting the General Characteristics to Particular Settings

Whatever the ranking of importance of the general characteristics, the critical factor is the ability to adapt selected characteristics to particular settings. Obviously many of the statements in the Preliminary List of Characteristics are extremely vague. Any two persons could not be expected to agree on what constitutes evidence that a facilitator "displays warmth, friendliness, and understanding with a wide variety of people," or "has charisma." The process of operationalization, described in Chapter V, strives to break down goals into directly observable component parts. This process (Appendix B) seems to be critical if the findings of this study are to be worthwhile. However, it would be futile to operationalize each statement in the Preliminary List since the List is intended as a suggestion bank and not as an ideal model. Individuals will not only need to choose specific statements with a particular situation in mind, they will need to operationalize those statements with the particular situation in mind as well. The following are selected skills, knowledge areas, and attitudes, which have been operationalized with a particular situation in mind.

Operationalized Statements

Situation A. A group of university students have formed a support group in order to prepare themselves to be facilitators of NFE. They review the Preliminary List of Characteristics and decide that "knows NFE from formal education" will be important. Using the operationalization process, they produce the following guidelines for themselves as facilitator trainees:

(a) can state general or theoretical reasons why it is important to know NFE from formal education;

(b) can cite practical reasons why a facilitator should know NFE from formal education;

(c) can cite a variety of general characteristics of NFE usually found in NFE programs;

(d) can state the particular characteristics that are important personally;

(e) can give reasons for accepting each of the personal characteristics of NFE;

(f) can give reasons for rejecting other characteristics suggested by peers or found in NFE literature;

(g) has observed a variety of NFE settings until familiar with each one so that extensive questioning about the setting can be answered;

(h) can relate case studies of other NFE programs;

(i) knows why each case cited is an NFE program (by own personal NFE characteristics);

(j) has taught in an NFE setting for a least one full week;

(k) has taught in a traditional classroom under a fairly demanding supervisor;

(l) has been a student in an NFE setting and in a formal
setting;

(m) can describe the difference in behaviors of a facilitator
and a traditional teacher (how each relates to students, peers,
and superiors; how each motivates others; how each fits into
the institution represented; what each says and does about
local and national realities; how each perceives the effect
the program has on learners; resources used by each; each's
perception of power within the institution; whether each is
learner centered, content centered, or teacher centered;
whether each gives tests and unsolicited evaluation; whether
each strives to be one of the learners);

(n) can observe a variety of educator roles and pick out
elements of NFE and elements of formal education;

(o) can role play a teacher and a facilitator;

(p) has role played enough times to feel comfortable in
each role and to be aware of the differences in each role;

(q) selects the appropriate role for different situations
articulating reasons for the selection;

(r) has received constructive criticism from peers on
personal performance as a facilitator;

(s) can describe an environment appropriate to NFE;

(t) can describe a traditional classroom to the satisfaction of a peer;

(u) can cite at least ten advantages and ten disadvantages of NFE and of the formal system;

(v) can state the difference between socialization and resocialization, explaining why the latter is more important to NFE;

(w) can state the difference between acculturation and enculturation, explaining why the former is more appropriate to NFE; and

(x) can articulate institutional differences between NFE and the formal system.

Situation B. Criteria are being developed to screen potential facilitators for mountain villages in Ecuador. The trainers and trainees all agree that "believes people should aspire to improve themselves and their community" is extremely important. When operationalized by the group the criteria is translated into the following behaviors or states:

(a) has helped organize community projects;

(b) has helped work on community projects;

(c) can articulate goals for the community whereby it would become more self-determining;

(d) does not attribute all social differences to fate or divine will;

(e) is not afraid to dialogue with officials and superiors;

(f) wants his children to be educated; and

(g) desires no financial reward for facilitator activities.

Situation C. A 4-H Club livestock project leader is demonstrating how to make a rope halter for younger members. The leader wishes to demonstrate skill in pacing during the demonstration. The following behaviors or states are identified as important in demonstrating this skill:

(a) knows the steps in making a rope halter;

(b) has experience in making the rope halter;

(c) plans presentation in advance;

(d) is well organized;

(e) has rehearsed the steps;

(f) limits the size of the group so that he can keep track of each individual;

(g) has materials ready so no interruptions will occur;

(h) has setting arranged where no interruptions will occur;

(i) gets the attention of everyone at the start;

(j) generates enthusiasm by showing the importance of the skill;

(k) uses visuals to demonstrate each step;

(l) is pleasant, enthusiastic, personable with each learner;

(m) makes sure each participant understands each step before proceeding to the next step;

(n) notes non-verbal behavior which indicates a lack of understanding, boredom;

(o) asks for questions;

(p) if someone is stuck and the leader is helping another, he asks a participant who is ahead of the group to help the stuck person;

(q) summarizes;

(r) evaluates to see that each person can make a rope halter; and

(s) has participants teach skill to a second group (one on one).

Situation D. In Toroko, a mountain village in Taiwan which is inhabited by the Atayal people, a facilitator from that village is being trained to "discover and articulate the learning needs present in the community." This skill is expressed in the following operationalized statements:

(a) articulates a number of ways in which markets outside the village cheat members of his village;

(b) demonstrates sufficient numerical skill to describe the process and outcome of market transactions;

(c) expresses a sense of individual and cultural identity;

(d) describes the institutions which his people must deal with;

(e) role-plays the behavior of officials which his people must deal with;

(f) articulates the values of the outside culture;

(g) articulates the values of his own culture;

(h) expresses some personal values which are not typical in his culture yet do not offend people in his culture;

(i) specifies unconventional uses for objects in his culture;

(j) specifies uses for objects which are available but are not commonly found in his culture;

(k) is willing to consider the feasability of untried courses of action;

(l) has the trust and respect of the community;

(m) asks open-ended questions whereby people talk about themselves and their community;

(n) listens without interrupting while people talk;

(o) indicates through non-verbal behavior that he understands and sympathizes with individuals;

(p) suggests non-traditional courses of action without alienating people;

(q) accepts and follows the suggestions of others;

(r) encourages people to talk to each other about community and individual problems;

(s) translates general dissatisfactions into specific solveable problems;

(t) records social, political, and ethical contradictions
present in the community;

(u) through questioning leads people to articulate an image
of their community after a particular problem has been
removed; and

(v) encourages others to discover and articulate the learning
needs present in the community.

Without doubt the ability to discover and articulate the learning needs
present in the community overlaps with other characteristics especially the
following: community planning; analytical skill; sensitivity to others; non-
verbal communication; discussion and dialogue skill; questioning skill;
ability to develop a communication network; awareness of what other
communities have done; and belief in the possibility of change and in people's
need to change. These general skills may need to be operationalized in order
to more fully understand how to discover and articulate the learning needs
present in the community.

It is anticipated that a facilitator may not be able to perform all of the
behaviors listed for this situation. He will, however, have concrete ideas
about how to discover and articulate learning needs present in the community.
Furthermore, a trainer or supervisor will have concrete ideas about how to
support the facilitator as he employs the general skill.

Summary

The Preliminary List of Characteristics, compiled from the literature review and Chapter I, provides a large number of skills, knowledge, and attitudes, thought relevant for facilitators of NFE. Questionnaires II and III were the consensus-forming part of the Delphi in which the items from the Preliminary List were rated by experts. A group modal consensus emerged in Questionnaire II. In Questionnaire III the group opinion became much stronger and a majority consensus can be found on all except one item. An analysis of the responses to Questionnaire III reveals extremely little disagreement among subgroups of experts. There is, in fact, strong agreement among the experts on the ratings.

Two comparison groups, with similar experience as the experts but with little or no knowledge of the Ecuador NFE Project, also rated the items. The comparison groups agree with the experts that virtually all of the skills, knowledge areas, and attitudes, are relevant to out-of-school educators. When the items are ranked on a continuum from most important to least important, differences occur among the three groups. Those differences are explained, to a large degree, by the experience and rhetoric of working on the Ecuador Project.

Finally a process is demonstrated whereby the general skills, knowledge, and attitudes, can be stated as particular behaviors. Since those behaviors depend on a specific setting, selected examples of skills, knowledge areas,

and attitudes, have been stated as specific behaviors for selected settings.

CHAPTER VII

SUMMARY AND CONCLUSIONS

Summary

The research questions posed in the introduction of this study have been answered. The nature of nonformal education has been discussed. The evolution of the facilitator idea in the Ecuador NFE Project has been traced and its weaknesses have been examined. Literature related to NFE and the Ecuador Project has been reviewed for implications to improve the facilitator idea. The general skills, knowledge, and attitudes of effective facilitators have been compiled and a process which yields observable behaviors from the general characteristics has been demonstrated.

Coombs' general definition of NFE has been used with the condition that certain dimensions must be considered and either included with the definition or rejected. My position is that the dimensions will vary according to the individual(s) using them and according to the particular NFE program, activity, or goal under consideration. The dimensions of NFE which are important to the focus of this study--NFE facilitators in community-based learning groups-- have been outlined and discussed.

The evolution of the facilitator idea in the Ecuador NFE Project has been examined and the findings of three major evaluation efforts which discern the weaknesses of the facilitator idea in the Project have been cited. Also literature on community development and teacher effectiveness was reviewed to discover implications for improving the facilitator idea. From the review of literature and responses to a brainstorm questionnaire (Questionnaire I) received from experts, a preliminary list of characteristics of effective facilitators in community-based learning groups has been assembled. This list includes the general skills, knowledge, and attitudes of effective facilitators as well as more specific statements which help clarify the general characteristics (Appendix A).

The general skills, knowledge, and attitudes have been submitted to the scrutiny of a panel of thirteen experts in the form of a Delphi questionnaire. The Delphi actually consists of three questionnaires: (a) a brainstorm questionnaire to elicit the general skills, knowledge, and attitudes; (b) Questionnaire II which asked the experts to rate the importance of each general skill, knowledge area, or attitude and (c) Question- naire III which gave feedback on the individual and group responses to Questionnaire II and asked for a reassessment of the responses.

The experts expressed a group opinion of the relative importance of each general skill, knowledge, and attitude. They also expressed whether each general characteristic is extremely important, important, preferable but not important, useful on occasion, or inappropriate for an effective facilitator. An expression of individual opinions which differ from the group opinion has also been elicited. The individual opinions are expressed as comments.

The opinion of the experts (staff members of the Ecuador NFE Project) was compared to the opinion of two other groups. Members of those comparison groups had experience in out-of-school educational activities but were not familiar with the Ecuador Project. In general the comparison groups confirm the relevance of virtually every item on the questionnaires. The comparison groups did disagree, at some points, with the experts on the relative importance of items. Those items which express learner-centered values, horizontal relationships, and individual differences, are favored by the experts. The comparison groups favor items which point toward more centralized control and responsibility on the part of the facilitator.

Finally, a process was proposed for reducing the general characteristics to directly observable behaviors or states. The process, operationalization of fuzzy concepts, was used to develop examples of behavioral statements for selected general characteristics in particular situations. These examples indicate how the other general characteristics can be reduced to directly observable behaviors or states for NFE activities in particular settings.

Conclusions

Most important selection criteria. Based on the findings of this study, the following general criteria are most important, according to the experts, for selecting Ecuadorian trainees to be facilitators of NFE in community-based learning groups:

(a) The facilitator should possess a strong sense of cultural pride.

(b) He should be flexible and creative.

(c) He should be dynamic and open.

(d) He should be available.

(e) His life style should not conflict with the community.

(f) He should believe that people ought to constantly aspire to improve themselves and their community.

(g) He should understand the nature of potential work in the community.

All of the other fifteen criteria are important or preferable except "has considerable schooling" which is inappropriate according to the experts.

Most important facilitator characteristics after training. According to the same experts the most important characteristics of Ecuadorian facilitators after training are:

(a) The facilitator should be skilled at discussion and dialogue.

(b) He should be able to increase people's confidence.

(c) He should be skilled in aiding community planning.

(d) He should be able to bring people together.

(e) He should be sensitive to the feelings, attitudes, and relationships of people.

(f) He should believe in the strength of shared decision making.

(g) He should be able to effect horizontal relationships.

(h) He should be skilled in dealing with diverse individual needs and abilities.

(i) He should be able to catalyze cooperation among people.

(j) He should be skilled in negotiating.

(k) He should possess group dynamics skills.

(l) He should have analytical and evaluation skills.

(m) He should see development as a process of liberation from domination and dependence.

(n) He should believe in the possibility of change, in people's capacity to grow, and in people's potential.

(o) He should be able to discover and articulate the learning needs present in the community.

(p) He should delegate authority.

(q) He should be able to motivate.

All of the other twenty-seven characteristics are important or useful on occasion according to the panel.

There is no clear group opinion concerning community selection of facilitator trainees. The responses do not indicate a clear group preference for either a "democratic process" or the "method normally used to make decisions in that community." The experts' votes and their comments indicate that community selection is a situational variable and it is impossible to establish a preference for a procedure, even in general terms, for Ecuadorian communities.

Analysis of questionnaires. The comparison groups generally confirm the importance of the items ranked highly by the experts. There are differences in the rank order of items among the experts and the two comparison groups but the comparison groups agree that all except one of the 66 items is relevant to effective facilitators.

From administering the questionnaires and analyzing the responses, the investigator concludes that there is negligible polarization of opinion between Ecuadorian and Northamerican respondents. A majority of Ecuadorians feel that considerable schooling is preferable as a criteria for selecting facilitators. A majority of North Americans feel that considerable schooling is inappropriate as a criteria for selecting facilitators. However, such polarization is not evident in the responses to any other item on the final questionnaire. Nor is there polarization when groups are compared by ethnic background, academic background, or field experience. Apparently the experience of working for the Project is the overriding determinant of responses on the questionnaires. An analysis of the abstractness or concreteness of the items also failed to explain the ratings or rankings of the items. Apparently the rank and rating of each item has little to do with the specificity or generality of the statement.

The Delphi technique. As a part of this study the Delphi technique was implemented and its assumptions were tested. Apparently a Delphi questionnaire is an effective technique for clarifying a group's opinion. A majority consensus can be achieved which indicates the group's opinion while allowing minority opinions to be articulated. Various human factors which sometimes prevent a group consensus--individual dominance, social noise, and group pressure--can be controlled through the Delphi.

By using a brainstorm questionnaire for the first round of the Delphi the experts are allowed to generate the items. Therefore the experts are not "locked in" to a set of items which may not cover the subject being investigated. New insights can also be elicited by allowing the experts to add new items on Questionnaire II and even Questionnaire III. Furthermore by encouraging comments on "any aspect of the questionnaire" for all of the questionnaires of the Delphi new ideas, insights, and opinions may be gained.

As on previous Delphi studies this study confirms the observation that major convergence of opinion takes place after the experts are informed of the first group voting. In this study of facilitators the feedback was received as part of Questionnaire III. Little change of opinion would be anticipated in this study if a fourth questionnaire were given. This conclusion is based on the fact that a majority consensus was achieved on 98% of the items on

Questionnaire III as compared with 59% of the items on Questionnaire II.

Personal contact with respondents in administering a Delphi was important in this study. A high rate of return of questionnaires was achieved which strengthens this study. Followup is important on a Delphi because an expert who responds to all questionnaires except one is useless. The Delphi depends on the same panel of experts for all rounds.

A potential problem of Delphis in bilingual situations is communication. Care was taken in the translation and pilot testing for this study of Ecuadorian facilitators. However more stringent procedures (e.g., double blind translation) could have been employed.

Another question which was uncovered but not answered in this study is the strength of group consensus on a Delphi. An apparently strong consensus may in fact be only a "paper consensus." This doubt can only be resolved by testing a Delphi consensus in a practical application involving the same experts who formed the group consensus.

Although not a focus of this study, the use of a Delphi to improve interpersonal relations in a group became evident. A Delphi enables any individual's opinion to be compared to the group opinion. By such a comparison individual deviance can be identified and brought into the open. A group discussion might not permit the identification of individual deviance because the individual may decline to express a strong opinion. For this reason many hidden agendas are not revealed in group discussions. Hidden agendas are harder to maintain in a Delphi study where the individual is asked to respond to each item in a climate where the personalities of other group members are not directly influential.

A final conclusion regarding the Delphi technique is that larger groups of experts could be involved. Analysis of Delphi questionnaires could easily be conducted through computer programs currently available.

Implications for Application

The findings and conclusions of this study are potentially useful in several ways. The study may serve as a basis for the following activities related to the Ecuador Project: (a) catalyzing discussion with the intent of examining and elaborating Project policies, priorities, and objectives; (b) developing observation instruments for particular facilitator settings; (c) guiding efforts in facilitator follow-up and supervision; (d) Project evaluation; and (e) guiding training efforts. Furthermore these activities may be useful to groups trying to adapt the facilitator idea to new settings. Especially useful for such groups will be implications for designing training programs.

Discussion catalyst. The findings of this study should be seriously discussed by members of the Ecuador Project staff. Both the group concensus and the comments of respondents who disagree with the group opinion should be considered. One of the objectives of that discussion should be to sharpen staff understanding and agreement on present policies, priorities, and objectives. The findings and conclusions should also be important to the formulation of future policies, priorities, and objectives.

Observation instruments. General characteristics may be chosen and operationalized with the operational statements then incorporated into an observation checklist. Information gathered from the use of such a checklist might be extremely helpful in understanding more about facilitators in particular and NFE in general.

Followup and supervision. Field staff and supervisors might use parts of this study in responding to the needs of individual facilitators. For example, a facilitator might indicate problems in bringing people together for learning sessions. Together the facilitator and the supervisor could operationalize the general characteristic, "able to bring people together." Statements would be made about what the facilitator should do in that particular situation in order to bring people together. The statements would serve the facilitator in planning strategies and guiding behavior to bring people together. The statements would serve the supervisor as an observation instrument to note the facilitator's behavior as he tried to bring people together. After a period of observation agreeable to both individuals, they could analyze the facilitator's reactions and the supervisor's observations. Together, the two might develop new strategies to help the facilitators over-come problems in bringing people together. Then, the facilitator might be left alone to implement the new strategies. A later followup conference between supervisor and facilitator would determine if the problem has been solved or further observations or conferences are needed. This process is essentially the supervision process suggested by Goldhammer (1969).

Project evaluation. An observation instrument easily lends itself to evaluation. Once objectives have been established, the observation instruments can be developed to indicate the extent to which the objectives have been met. Particular evaluation questions might include the impact of different kinds of training and field support mechanisms, needs for inservice training and supervision, present individual and group interaction styles, changes in individuals and groups over time, and changes in institutions resulting from cooperation with facilitators or trainers.

Guiding training efforts. From their own experiences and from the Preliminary List of Characteristics, Project staff may identify problem areas or skills, knowledge, and attitudes which are presently overlooked in training facilitators. Once identified, the area or characteristic can be operationalized to produce a description of the behavior of a facilitator who is effective in that characteristic. The operationalized statements would indicate the experiences needed to acquire the skill, knowledge, or attitude in question. This process of developing a training program is very similar to the competency-based training approach.

Training facilitators for other settings. Individuals and institutions wishing to train facilitator-like educational leaders in other countries may be able to use this study as a point of departure. The Preliminary List of Characteristics together with a sensitivity for the social and cultural characteristics of the setting in question might be useful in formulating priorities, objectives, and guidelines for training. General skills, knowledge, and attitudes, important to local educators in NFE could be operationalized for the particular situation. Some of the general characteristics regarded as relevant for Ecuador may not be relevant for other settings. Also there may be general characteristics, important to facilitators in a particular setting, which are not on the Preliminary List. Even if the Preliminary List is not directly relevant for specific program needs, the list might be useful as a discussion catalyst to stimulate the identification of other characteristics.

General issues in application. When the results of this study are applied to particular settings in training new facilitators, problems will certainly emerge. Since the list of relevant characteristics is long, facilitators will not likely be trained in all relevant skills, knowledge areas, and attitudes. In many cases even all of the important skills may not be included. The question which arises is, "Which skills, knowledge areas, and attitudes, will be chosen?"

The choice of easily trainable skills and knowledge areas for training will be a temptation. Relatively concrete skills like questioning skill, non-verbal communication skill, and materials development skills, may be featured. While abstract skills and attitudes may be ignored. Another related problem is that abstract skills and attitudes may be dealt with in a very general and rhetorical manner. However the operationalization process provides an answer to both of these problems. Apparently vague and abstract concepts can be stated in observable behaviors which allows more concrete training experiences to be provided.

Another approach to dealing with training would be to divide the selected skills, knowledge, and attitudes, into priority groups. Group 1 could be the most important qualities of beginning facilitators. Group 2 skills, knowledge, and attitudes, would be those which could wait for a few months and then be provided through a short "refresher" course. Group 3 qualities might be those which inservice training, counseling, or support groups, could provide as the skill, information, or attitude, becomes important. Group 4 skills might be highly sophisticated or specialized skills. Only certain facilitators might be chosen for intensive training in these skills. By setting such priorities, however, training programs would not have to worry about all relevant facilitator characteristics at once.

Still another approach to training for many and diverse facilitator characteristics might be the team approach. Four or more facilitators might be chosen from one community. These facilitators would be chosen for differing yet complementary qualities. One pair might be trained for process skills and attitudes while the other pair is trained for task-oriented skills or knowledge relevant to particular tasks. Other divisions of skills might be made assuming a team of complementary facilitators.

Obviously training will depend on selection. If selection is rigorous and well done, the training will take a different form than training of facilitators where the selection must be uncontrolled by the trainers.

A final problem may be the use of the operationalization procedure. If time does not allow use of each step then a modified procedure may be used. The second, third, fourth and fifth steps may be ignored if necessary (see pp. 167-168).

Implications for further study

This study focused on Ecuador Project staff members as the experts. An important contribution to the Ecuador Project would be made if the Delphi part of the study were replicated using Ecuadorian facilitators and learners. The investigator's presence in Ecuador would be a prerequisite for such a study. Furthermore, the utility of the written Delphi questionnaires would be doubtful. Possibly an oral version of the Delphi technique would prove useful. Such a study would extend the findings of the study.

Another replication of the Delphi might be administered to U.S.A.I.D. staff in Ecuador and in Washington. Information acquired from this group could be compared with the responses of the Ecuador Project staff in order to facilitate communication between the two groups and to readjust present assumptions and expectations of each group which may be in conflict with each other.

This study suggests needs for university or professional staff working in NFE. An idea suggested by this study which needs to be developed is the consultant as facilitator. Also needed is a self-training model by which trainers could prepare themselves to train facilitators.

To more fully understand the similarities and differences between facilitators and teachers, a comparison of the facilitator characteristics with teacher characteristics would be interesting. Perhaps the facilitator could be compared with a "traditional" teacher role as well as an "open classroom" teacher role.

Perhaps the most important question raised by the study is, "Can the Preliminary List of Characteristics and the operationalization process be productively employed in developing a facilitator training program in another cultural setting?" The question will be answered only after such an attempt is made.

A Final Note

This study has produced ideas and a process which are potentially useful in developing NFE programs in diverse cultures. The study was not intended to produce a prescription or an ideal model by which such programs can be developed; nor has such a model been produced. The ideas and the process which result from this study are intended as convivial tools. Illich coined

the term

"conviviality" to designate the opposite of industrial
productivity. I intend it to mean autonomous and
creative intercourse among persons, and the intercourse of persons with their environment; and this
in contrast with the conditioned response of persons
to the demands made upon them by others and by a
man-made environment. I consider conviviality to
be individual freedom realized in personal interdependence and, as such, an intrinsic ethical
value. I believe that, in any society, as conviviality
is reduced below a certain level, no amount of
industrial productivity can effectively satisfy the
needs it creates among society's members
(Illich, 1973, p. 11).

BIBLIOGRAPHY

BIBLIOGRAPHY

Alschuler, A. "Concientization." Amherst, Mass.: School of Education, University of Massachusetts, 1972.

American Technical Assistance Corp. An evaluation of motivational training as used by AID in Latin America. Washington: A.T.A.C., 1971.

Amidon, E. J. "Interaction analysis." Unpublished.

Anderson, C. A. "Fostering and inhibiting factors." In Brembeck, C. A., New strategies for educational development. Lexington, Mass.: D. C. Heath, 1973.

Anderson, D. P. "Exploring the potential of the Delphi technique by analyzing the applications." An A.E.R.A. Symposium, Ohio State University, March, 1970.

Ashton-Warner, S. Teacher. New York: Simon and Schuster, 1963.

Axinn, G. H. Study team reports: Toward a strategy of interaction in nonformal education. East Lansing, Mich.: Michigan State University, 1974.

Axinn, G. & Thorat, S. Modernizing world agriculture: A comparative study for agricultural extension education systems. New York: Praeger, 1972.

Batten, T. R. School and community in the tropics. London: Oxford University Press, 1959.

Batten, T. R. Training for community development. London: Oxford University Press, 1962,

Batten, T. R. The human factor in community work. London: Oxford University Press, 1965.

Batten, T. R. The non-directive approach in group and community work. London: Oxford University Press, 1967.

Bell, R. E. Competency-based leadership: A conceptual model and case study. Amherst, Mass.: Center for International Education, University of Massachusetts, 1973.

Biddle, W. W. & Biddle, L. J. The community development process: The rediscovery of local initiative. New York: Holt, Rinehart & Winston, 1965.

Billimoria, R. "Indigenous patterns of education." Non-formal education in a world context. Amherst, Mass.: Center for International Education, University of Massachusetts, 1973.

Blanchard, K. & Hersey, P. Management of Organizational Behavior. Englewood Cliffs, N.J.: Prentice-Hall, 1969.

Bock, J. & Papagiannis, G. "The demystification of non-formal education: A social-psychological paradigm for a comparative study of non-formal education." Palo Alto, Calif.: Stanford International Development Center, Stanford University, 1973.

Bonilla, R., Laverty, N., Quintana, A., Suero, J., & Wilhelm, R. "Sabaneta: Beyond negation--finding a critical consciousness." Risk. Geneva, Switzerland: World Council of Churches, Vol. 6, No. 4, 1970.

Bradfield, D. J. Guide to extension training. Rome: Food & Agricultural Organization of the United Nations, 1966.

Bradford, L. P., Gibb, J. R. & Benne, K. D. T-group theory and laboratory method. New York: John Wiley & Sons, 1964,

Brager, G. A. & Purchell, F. P. Community action against poverty. New Haven, Conn.: College and University Press, 1967.

Brembeck, C. S. New strategies for educational development: The cross-cultural search for nonformal alternatives. Lexington, Mass.: D. C. Heath, 1973.

Callaway, A. "Frontiers of out-of-school education." In Brembeck, C. S., New Strategies for educational development. Lexington, Mass.: D. C. Heath, 1973

Campbell. Quoted in Carey, D. M. An assessment of the future inservice training needs of school principals in Massachusetts: A Delphi study. Amherst, Mass.: University of Massachusetts, 1972.

Carey, D. M. An assessment of the future inservice training needs of school principals in Massachusetts: A Delphi study. Amherst, Mass.: University of Massachusetts, 1972.

Center for Curriculum Design (ed.). Somewhere else. Chicago: Swallow Press, 1973.

Cerych, L. Problems of aid to education in developing countries. New York: Praeger, 1965.

Charnofsky, S. Educating the powerless. Belmont, Calif.: Wadsworth, 1971.

Clinic to Improve University Teaching. "Teaching analysis by students (TABS)." Amherst, Mass.: School of Education, University of Massachusetts, 1973.

Coffing, R. T., Hutchinson, T. E., Thomann, J. B. & Allan, R. G. "Self-instructional module for learning the Hutchinson method of operationalizing a goal or intent." Amherst, Mass.: University of Massachusetts, 1971.

Combs, A. "Fostering self-direction." In Howes, V. M., Individualization of instruction: A teaching strategy. London: Macmillan, 1970.

Combs, A., Avila, D. & Purkey, W. W. Helping relationships: Basic concepts for the helping professions. Boston: Allyn & Bacon, 1973.

Coombs, P. The world educational crisis. New York: Oxford University Press, 1968.

Coombs, P. New paths to learning for rural children and youth. New York: International Council for Educational Development, 1973.

Coombs, P. & Ahmed, M. Attacking rural poverty: How nonformal education can help. Baltimore, Md.: The Johns Hopkins University Press, 1974.

Coombs, P. Building new educational strategies to serve rural children and youth. In press.

Council for Social Development. Action for rural change: Readings in Indian community development. New Delhi: Munshiram Manoharlal, 1970.

Cyphert, F. R. & Gant, W. L. "The Delphi technique: A case study." Phi Delta Kappa, January, 1971.

Dale, E. Building a learning environment. Bloomington, Ind.: Phi Delta Kappa, 1972.

Dalkey, N. C. The Delphi method: An experimental study of group opinion. The Rand Corporation, RM-5883-PR, June, 1969.

Dalkey, N. C. "Predicting the future." In Carey, D. M. An assessment of the future inservice training needs of school principals in Massachusetts: A Delphi study. Amherst, Mass.: University of Massachusetts, 1972.

Dalkey, N. C. & Helmer, O. "An experimental application of the Delphi method to the use of experts." Management Science, April, 1963.

Dalton, G. (ed.). Economic development and social change. Garden City, New York: The natural History Press, 1971.

"Education for awareness: A talk with Paulo Freire." Risk. Geneva, Switzerland: World Council of Churches, Vol. 6, No. 4, 1970.

Elam, S. "Performance-based teacher education: What is the state of the art?" Washington: American Association of Colleges for Teacher Education, 1971.

Etling, A. "Chapare: A team approach to the new educational challenge in Bolivia's jungles." New World Outlook, November, 1972.

Evans, D. & Etling, A. "Don't look now Chairman Mao: We're preparing facilitators to be nonformal educators." Meforum, Fall, 1974.

Evans, D. & Hoxeng, J. "The Ecuador Project: Technical note no. 1." Amherst, Mass.: Center for International Education, University of Massachusetts, 1972.

Evans, D. & Smith, W. "Nonformal education: The light at the end of the tunnel." Nonformal education in a world context. Amherst, Mass.: Center for International Education, University of Massachusetts, 1973.

Faure, E. <u>Learning to be.</u> Paris: UNESCO, 1972.

Fiedler, F. <u>A theory of leadership effectiveness</u>. New York: McGraw Hill, 1967.

Figueroa, P. "Informe final de la evaluacion del proyecto de educaion no formal." Quito, Ecuador: Centro de Motivacion y Asesoria, 1972.

Flanders, N. A. <u>Interaction analysis in the classroom</u>. Ann Arbor, Mich.: University of Michigan, 1966.

Freire, P. <u>Education como practica de la libertad.</u> Montevideo: Tierra Nueva, 1969.

Freire, P. <u>Pedagogy of the oppressed.</u> New York: Herder and Herder, 1972.

Gillette, A. "Review of Ecuador Project Film." <u>Prospects:</u> Quarterly review of education, Vol. IV, No. 1, Spring, 1974.

Goldhammer, R. <u>Clinical supervision.</u> New York: Holt, Rinehart and Winston, 1969.

Gordon, J. W. <u>My country school diary</u>. New York: Dell, 1970.

Gordon, T. J. & Ament, R. H. <u>Forecasts of some technological and scientific developments and their societal consequences</u>. Institute for the Future, 1969.

Grandstaff, M. "Nonformal education and an expanded conception of development." <u>Nonformal education discussion papers.</u> East Lansing, Mich.: Michigan State University, 1973.

Gunter, J. "Ashton-Warner literacy method: Technical note no. 5." Amherst, Mass.: Center for International Education, University of Massachusetts, 1973.

Hamachek, D. "Characteristics of good teachers & implications for teacher education." <u>Phi Delta Kappan,</u> February, 1969.

Harbison, F. H. "Human resources and nonformal education." In Brembeck, C. S. <u>New strategies for educational development.</u> Lexington, Mass.: D. C. Heath, 1973.

Harmon, M. "Key concepts of Paulo Friere: Their meaning & implications for United States education." Unpublished manuscript. Center for Humanistic Education, University of Massachusetts.

Helmer, O. The use of the Delphi technique in problems of educational innovations. Rand Corporation, December, 1966.

Hersey, P. Management concepts and behavior: Programmed instruction for managers. Little Rock, Arkansas: Marvern Publishing Co., 1967.

Hilliard, J. F. "Elements of an action program." In Brembeck, C. S., New strategies for educational development. Lexington, Mass.: D. C. Heath, 1973.

Holt, J. What do I do Monday? New York: Dell, 1970.

Horowitz, I. The rise and fall of project camelot: Studies in the relationship between social science and practical politics. Cambridge, Mass.: The M.I.T. Press, 1967.

Houghton, H. & Tregear, P. (eds.). Community schools in developing countries. New York: UNESCO Institute for Education, 1969.

Howes, V. M. Individualization of instruction: A teaching strategy. London: Macmillan, 1970.

Hoxeng, J. "Hacienda: Technical note no. 3." Amherst, Mass.: Center for International Education, University of Massachusetts, 1972.

Hoxeng, J. Let Jorge do it: An approach to rural nonformal education. Amherst, Mass.: Center for International Education, University of Massachusetts, 1973.

Ickis, V. "A new approach to community education." Amherst, Mass.: Center for International Education, University of Massachusetts, 1972.

Illich, I. Deschooling society. New York: Harper & Row, 1970.

Illich, I. Tools for conviviality. New York: Harper & Row, 1973.

Jones, A. D. "Social and psychological factors in teaching farmers." Human Organization. Vol. 33, No. 1, Spring, 1974.

Kansas Extension Service. "A guide to extension programs for Kansas." Manhattan, Kansas: Extension Service, Kansas State University, 1960.

Kenyatta, J. Facing Mt. Kenya. New York: Random House, 1965.

King, C. Working with the people in community action. New York: Association Press, 1965.

King, J. "Planning non-formal education in Tanzania." Paris UNESCO-International Institute for Educational Planning, 1967.

Kleis, J., Lang, L., Mietus, J. R. & Tiapula, F. T. S. "Toward a contextual definition of nonformal education." Nonformal education discussion papers. East Lansing, Mich.: Michigan State University, 1973.

Knaus, K. Notebook in extension history, objectives & staff functions. Stillwater, Okla.: Oklahoma Agricultural & Mechnical College, 1955.

Kohl, H. Thirty-six children. New York: The New American Library, 1968.

Laubach, F. C. & Laubach, R. S. Toward world literacy: The each one teach one way. Syracuse, N.Y.: Syracuse University Press, 1960.

Leonard, G. B. Education & ecstasy. New York: Dell, 1968.

Lindsay, C. "The 4-H project leader." Columbia, Mo.: Extension Division University of Missouri, 1972.

McNamara, R. S. "Address to the board of governors." Nairobi, Kenya: World Bank, 1973.

Melnik, M. A. The development & analysis of a clinic to improve university teaching. Amherst, Mass.: University of Massachusetts, 1972.

Menkerios, H. "Agricultural Extension Services." Essex, Conn." International Council for Educational Development, 1972.

Millwood, D. "Conscientization: What it's all about." New Internationalist. June, 1974.

Missouri Extension Service. "4-H club leaders manual." Columbia, Mo.: University Extension Division, University of Missouri, 1969.

Missouri Extension Service. "Missouri's guide to 4-H leadership development." Columbia, Mo.: University Extension Division, University of Missouri, 1968.

Montgomery, G. "Education and training for agricultural development." Symposium volume on Agricultural and Economic Development.

Nash, H. W. "Games for living." War on hunger. Washington: Agency for International Development, December, 1973.

Neill, A. S. Summerhill. New York: Hart, 1960.

Newbry, B. & Applegate, S. "The nonformal education project in Ecuador conducted by the University of Massachusetts." Washington: United States Agency for International Development, April 9, 1973.

Nonformal alternatives to schooling: A glossary of educational methods. Amherst, Mass.: Center for International Education, University of Massachusetts, 1972.

Nonformal education, A.I.D. Bibliography Series. Washington, D.C.: Agency for International Development, 1971.

Nyerere, J. "Education for self-reliance." Speech. Dar es Salaam, 1967.

Nylen, D., Mitchell, J. & Strout, A. Handbook of staff development and human relations training. Washington: NTL Institute for Applied Behavioral Science, 1967.

Office of Education. Seeing education whole. Geneva, Switzerland: World Council of Churches, 1970.

Paik, H. K. "Nonformal education in Korea: Programs and prospects." In Brembeck, C. S., New strategies for educational development. Lexington, Mass.: D. C. Heath, 1973.

Paulston, R. G. (ed.). Nonformal education: An annotated international bibliography. New York: Praeger, 1972.

Paulston, R. G. "Nonformal educational alternatives." In Brembeck, C. S., New strategies for educational development. Lexington, Mass.: D. C. Heath, 1973(a).

Paulston, R. G. "The 'shadow school system' in Peru." In Brembeck, C. S. New strategies for educational development. Lexington, Mass.: D. C. Heath, 1973(b).

Pfieffer, J. New look at education. Princeton, N.J.: Western Publishing Co., 1968.

Piveteau, J. Guide pour votre ecole de promotion collective. Paris: CEPAM, 1972.

Plan quinquenal de educacion funcional de adultos, 1973-77. Quito, Ecuador: Ministry of Education, 1972.

Postman, N. & Weingarter, C. Teaching as a subversive activity. New York: Delcorte Press, 1969.

Postman, N. & Weingarter, C. The soft revolution. New York: Dell, 1971.

Raper, A. F. Rural development in action: The comprehensive experiment at Comilla, East Pakistan. Ithaca, N.Y.: Cornell University Press, 1970.

Reed, D. "Conscientization: An experience in Peru." New Internationalist. June, 1974.

Reimer, E. An essay on alternatives in education: Cuaderno No. 1005. Cuernavaca, Mexico: Centro Internacional de Documentacion, 1970.

Reisser, L. J. A facilitator process for self-directed learning. Amherst, Mass.: University of Massachusetts, 1973.

Rogers, C. R. Freedom to learn. Columbus, Ohio: Charles E. Merrill, 1969.

Rogers, E. & Schoemaker, F. Communication of innovations: A cross-cultural approach. New York: The Free Press, 1971.

Schindler-Rainman, E. & Lippitt, R. The volunteer community. Washington: Center for a Voluntary Society, National Training Laboratories, 1971.

Schoolboys of Barbiana. Letter to a teacher. New York: Random House, 1971.

Schmuch, R. A. & Schmuck, P. A. Group processes in the classroom. Dubuque, Iowa: William C. Brown, 1971.

Schrank, J. Teaching human beings. Boston: Beacon Press, 1972.

Scriven, M. "The methodology of evaluation." Unpublished.

Sheffield, J. R. & Diejomaoh, P. Nonformal education in African development. New York: African American Institute, 1973.

Silvert, K. H. "Ethics and programmatic thinking about rural welfare." Mexico City: Ford Foundation, 1972.

Simon, A. & Boyer, E. G. "Mirrors for behavior: An anthology of classroom observation instruments." Philadelphia: Research for Better Schools, 1967.

Simon, S., Howe, L. W., & Kirschenbaum, H. Values clarification. New York: Hart, 1972.

Spector, P. "Communication media and motivation in the adoption of new practices: An experiment in rural Ecuador." Human Organization. Vol. 30, No. 1, Spring, 1971.

Smith, W. "Consientizacao and simulation games: Technical note no. 2." Amherst, Mass.: Center for International Education, University of Massachusetts, 1972.

Stake, R. E. "Generalization of program evaluation: The need for limits." Educational Product Report, Vol. 2, No. 5, February, 1969.

"Stanford teacher competence appraisal guide." Unpublished.

Stufflebeam, D. (ed.). Educational evaluation and decision making. Bloomington, Ind.: Phi Delta Kappa, 1971.

Subcommittee on Scope and Responsibility. "The Cooperative Extension Service today." Washington: Federal Extension Service, 1958.

Swanson, D. A. The University of Massachusetts project: An evaluation of nonformal education in Ecuador. Quito, Ecuador: U. S. Agency for International Development, 1973.

Team Leadership Development Project. Perspectives on the role of the Teacher Corps team leader. Toledo: University of Toledo, 1971.

The O. M. Collective. The organizer's manual. New York: Bantam Books, 1971.

Twenty-four Group methods and techniques for adult education (ERIC) ED 024 882.

University of Massachusetts Teacher Corps. Minimal competencies for teaching interns: A performance-based teacher education model. Amherst, Mass.: University of Massachusetts, 1973.

Waldera, D. R. Anticipated roles of future educators: A Delphi study. Amherst, Mass.: University of Massachusetts, 1971.

Ward, T. "The why and how of evaluation in nonformal education." East Lansing, Mich.: Michigan State University, 1973.

Ward, T., Dettoni, J. & McKinney, L. "Designing effective learning in non-formal modes." In Brembeck, C. A., New strategies for educational development. Lexington, Mass.: D. C. Heath, 1973.

Weaver, T. W. The Delphi method: Background and critique. New York: Educational Research Center, Syracuse University, 1971.

Weaver, T. W. The Delphi forecasting method." Phi Delta Kappan, January, 1971.

Weigand, J. B. (ed.). Developing teacher competencies. Englewood Cliffs, N. J.: Prentice-Hall, 1971.

"What's happening in Ecuador." The Christian Science Monitor. Wednesday, February 13, 1974.

Wight, A. R. & Hammons, M. A. Guidelines for Peace Corps cross-cultural training, part 1. Estes Park, Colo.: Center for Research and Education, 1970.

Wilhelms, F. "Educational conditions essential to growth in individuality."
In Howes, V. M., Individualization of instruction: A teaching strategy.
London: Macmillan, 1970.

Williams, R. "Towards a pedagogy of oppressed youth." Convergence.
Vol. IV, No. 2, 1971.

Willner, Dorothy. "Community leadership." In Council of Social Development, Action for rural change: Readings in Indian community development. New Delhi: Munshiram Manoharlal, 1970.

World survey of education, Volume V. New York: UNESCO, 1971.

Unpublished Ecuador Project Documents

1. Andrade, D. "Field notes on Columbe/Colonche."

2. Barriga, P. "Memorandum no. 39: Plan of action."

3. "Contract between the United States of America and the University of Massachusetts, No. AID/1a-699 (Ecuador)." January 1, 1972.

4. Etling, A. "Summary of project evaluation efforts." June 1, 1973.

5. Evans, D. R., Etling, A. & Gunter, J. "An approach to evaluation of the nonformal education project in Ecuador."

6. Forman, S. "Report on the evaluation study of the Colta/Columbe facilitator project." April 15, 1974.

7. Fotonovelas:
   a. "Entre el amour y la esperanza."
   b. "El caso de la mancha de aji."
   c. "De quien es nuestra tierra?"
   d. "Agua que no has de beber."

8. Ochoa, A. "Third year proposal, Ecuador Project." January 29, 1974.

9. Project Staff. "Project evaluation report 1."

10. Project Staff. "Annex to final report." May 1, 1973.

11. Project Staff. "Evaluation of U.S.A.I.D./Ecuador-M.O.E. Community education project."

12. Project Staff. "Field notes on original facilitator communities."

13. Project Staff. "Final report." December, 1972.

14. Project Staff. "Final report." February 1, 1973.

15. Project Staff. "Mid-year report." August 1, 1972.

16. Project Staff. "Second six-month report." October 24, 1973.

17. Project Staff. "Six-month report." July, 1972.

18. Project Staff. "Summary year-long work plan." April 1, 1973- March 31, 1974.

19. Project Staff. "Third quarter work plan." December, 1973.

20. Smith, W., Tasiguano, E. & Moreno, C. "A facilitator selection workshop." August, 1974.

21. Ward, T. "Evaluation plan for the University of Massachusetts project/ nonformal education." August, 1973.

APPENDIX A

PRELIMINARY LIST OF FACILITATOR

CHARACTERISTICS

Preliminary List of Facilitator Characteristics

These items are the result of the review of literature and the responses to Questionnaire I. Those items suggested by the panel of experts are followed by an asterisk. The items have been grouped into general categories which were divided into two lists: criteria for selecting facilitator trainees and characteristics of facilitators after training.

Criteria for Selecting Facilitator Trainees

A. Background

    1. Stable personal and family situation*
      a. mature mentally and physically. *
      b. stable emotionally and economically. *
      c. low in anxiety.
      d. accepts self and others.
      e. resident of the community. *
      f. secure, strong ties in the community. *
      g. married, or living with the family.
      h. healthy, not dominated by drink. *
      i. skilled in carrying on some kind of work.
      j. fairly young.
      k. Possesses self-confidence. *

    2. Experience in civic and community affairs. *
      a. is a member of the community. *
      b. knows the territory. *
      c. participates in the culture of the community. *
      d. acquainted with local resources.
      e. knows people's beliefs, values, and customs as well as their relationships and attitudes towards each other.
      f. has a fairly clear perspective of the economic and social situation of community members. *
      g. active in civic and community affairs. *
      h. member of various groups and organizations.
      i. has demonstrated interest in community development.
      j. has community organization experience and ability. *
      k. likes to work in groups, can guide groups. *
      l. has some experience external to the village. *

3. Life style does not conflict with the community.*
   a. speaks the language of the majority.*
   b. advocates the culture of the community.*
   c. close to learners in education, economic level, social distance, and physical distance.
   d. not afraid of hard manual labor.

4. Proven leader*
   a. has previously demonstrated leadership qualities.*
   b. has charisma (elusive charm, magnetism, persuasive power, and the capacity to excite and inspire others).*
   c. is strengthened by a strongly held conviction which is beneficial to the followers.

5. Respected and accepted by a wide variety of community members.*
   a. has friendly personal relations with people in the community.
   b. is accepted by the major subgroups of the community.
   c. has at least tacit support of existing leadership in the community.*
   d. is not a reactionary nor too far out.*
   e. distinguished in the village.
   f. has credibility in the eyes of the students.
   g. is trusted.
   h. has status, prestige, and esteem.

B. Personality

1. Dynamic and open*
   a. active, alert, and energetic.*
   b. interested in new ideas, seeks our information.
   c. shows initiative, is reasonably aggressive.*
   d. ambitious but not egoistic.*
   e. active but stimulates others to act.*
   f. open to new proposals, experience, change; not afraid of "crazy" ideas.*
   g. accepts the unknown; is not upset by the unexpected.
   h. is spontaneous.
   i. often takes calculated risks.
   j. intelligent and articulate.
   k. has charisma--personality force.*
   l. has abandoned passivity and fatalism.
   m. shows continued freshness of appreciation.
   n. enjoys mystic experience (strong emotional response of wonder, ecstasy, limitless horizons).

o. avoids behind-the-scenes manipulation.
p. is honest and authentic in dealing with others.
q. is relatively non-defensive.
r. not a representative for a faction or clique. *
s. is not blindly loyal to a particular institution. *

2. Independent yet cooperative*
   a. not submissive to authority. *
   b. independent from authority of traditional figures. *
   c. autonomous (independent of culture and environment).
   d. does not accept the status quo. *
   e. has ideas different from the majority, diverse, unconventional. *
   f. has an "inner directedness" of conviction that holds to own values; strength of character.
   g. resists dependency-producing situations.

3. Flexible and creative*
   a. pliable, can change goals according to the circumstances. *
   b. is adaptable and able to improvise.
   c. possesses a high tolerance for ambiguity.
   d. divergent and creative in behavior and attitude. *
   e. basic intelligence. *
   f. original thought.
   g. detachment, need for privacy.
   h. informal.
   i. relates easily. *

4. Organized and dependable*
   a. likes order and correctness; carefully plans own affairs.
   b. enjoys organizing to make things happen. *
   c. is disciplined and conscientious. *
   d. honest, reliable, punctual; carries out responsibilities. *
   e. possesses common sense and good judgment. *
   f. patient and persistent yet not narrow minded. *
   g. has a sense of self-direction.
   h. non-partisan, humble, devoted to people; on the side of the good that is shared by all.
   i. problem centering rather than self-centering.
   j. rhetoric is minimal. *

5. Likeable*
   a. pleasant, friendly, approachable, congenial.*
   b. natural; warm towards people.
   c. has a social style that does not offend people.*
   d. philosophical, unhostile sense of humor.*
   e. gregarious and does not preach.*
   f. is not grouchy or sarcastic.

C. Knowledge

1. Literacy and numeracy*
   a. can read, write, and do math.*
   b. has minimal literacy skills.*

2. Keeps up with local, regional and national news.

3. Understands the nature of potential work in the community.
   a. is aware of the responsibilities.
   b. is aware of the significance of the work.

D. Attitudes

1. Sensitive, considerate, and open to people from different backgrounds.*
   a. communicates with different ages, sexes, and statuses in the village.*
   b. relates to different people as well as religious and political authorities.*
   c. employs horizontal communications between people.*
   d. feels equal to others and makes others feel equal.*
   e. facilitates communication among people.*
   f. facilitates community decisions with a broad base of input.*
   g. involves people in decisions.*
   h. listens.*
   i. displays warmth, friendliness and understanding with a wide variety of people.
   j. likes people, strives for deeper personal relationships; is sentimental.*
   k. is able to empathize with others.
   l. can see things from the other person's point of view.
   m. patient, non-partisan, devoted to people, on the side of the common good.
   n. has a feeling for mankind--an identification with and sympathy for the human race; desires to help.

o. discriminates between means and ends.
p. is helpful in interpersonal relationships.
q. perceptive of group dynamics.*
r. has the capacity to learn from anyone who has something to teach.
s. constantly seeks to increase own sensitivity.
t. is authentic and has a positive view of self and others.
u. responsive to criticism.*
v. understands exploitive relationships and solutions to them.*
w. is firm without being authoritarian.*
x. emphasizes just, humane, respectful treatment of subordinates.
y. advocates human rights.*

2. Believes people should constantly aspire to improve themselves and their communities.
   a. sincerely desires to help the community improve.
   b. advocates community development.*
   c. has directions in mind whereby the community will become self-determining.*
   d. believes in change.*
   e. is optimistic about one's ability to direct one's life.*
   f. wants to improve personally but has no illusions about becoming rich.
   g. is eager to learn.*
   h. is ambitious.
   i. asks questions.*
   j. is a good neighbor who is always ready to help.
   k. displays an attitude of social responsibility.
   l. has a sense of mission--an ideal of service.
   m. neither asks for nor expects financial reward.*
   n. dedicated and zealous.
   o. not submissive to authorities.*

3. Possesses strong beliefs in the potential of NFE*
   a. has goals for the community which can be attacked by NFE.*
   b. believes in decision-making at the local level.*

E. Other

1. Available*
   a. does not have other obligations which conflict with facilitator responsibilities.

249

  b. interested, motivated, willing.*
  c. accepts responsibilities.
  d. able to work at least two months on the project each year.

2. Selected by the community*
   a. is chosen by a large proportion of the community to be
      represented.
   b. selected by peers in the community and is subject to dismissal
      by them.*
   c. is selected by the community using its own criteria.*
   d. is selected by a democratic process.
   e. accountable to the members of the community.*

Characteristics of Facilitators After Training

A. Communication and Interpersonal (Facilitators' direct and overt intervention in the learning groups)

1. Speaking skills. *
    a. communicates simply but effectively
    b. is specific.
    c. clarifies ideas or materials which need elaboration.

2. Questioning skills*
    a. asks questions that are easily understood.
    b. asks thought provoking questions.
    c. uses open-ended questions.
    d. asks questions which lead group to reflect on or discuss community problems. *
    e. asks questions about the reality in which we live. *
    f. looks for incongruities.
    g. presents a model of critical questioning. *
    h. encourages questioning.
    i. questions participants in order to make their views clearer to the group.
    j. uses informal one-to-one discussion interview.
    k. interviews to elicit creative expression for taped vignettes, radio-novelas, drama. *
    l. waits for answers. *
    m. answers questions clearly and concisely.

   Discussion and Dialogue skills
    a. listens attentively to others. *
    b. does not dominate. *
    c. recognizes differences in opinions and accepts them.
    d. nonverbal communication skill (posture, facial expression, gesture, etc.)
    f. looks for disagreement in the expressions of silent members
    g. introduces new ideas--contributes relevant points.
    h. summarizes main points, progress, and unfinished work, and shows relationships among ideas or suggestions. *
    i. relates discussion to practical situation.
    j. sums up and integrates the comments of others-- paraphrases.

k. poses open-ended problems.
l. gives and asks for suggestions.
m. checks for agreement.
n. encourages participants to respond to each others' ideas.
o. helps clarify unclear statements made by others.
p. encourages lively communications.
q. encourages a mutual learning process.
r. facilitates sounding of opinions. *
s. provides structure.
t. keeps discussion focused on one item at a time.
u. describes own feelings.
v. checks own perceptions orally for clarity.
w. shares agendas. *
x. checks the feelings others.
y. attends to feelings involved in the dialogue process.
z. contributes to the personal feelings of security in participaints.
aa. absorbs or drains off feelings of threat.
bb. checks for hidden assumptions and biases.
cc. makes people aware of needs which they are not fully aware of.
dd. helps evaluate progress.

4. Analytical and Evaluation skills*

a. presents a model of critical questioning. *
b. draws out general conclusions to guide future work.
c. encourages consideration of every question.
d. helps people think more systematically and objectively about themselves and others.
e. persists in spite of failure to find a better solution.
f. knows that oppression is not simply the situation itself, but it is also the perception of the situation by the oppressed.
g. recognizes ignorance (own as well as others').
h. gives positive feedback frequently.
i. encourages asking for feedback frequently.
j. develops and uses effective feedback devices.
k. gives and receives feedback.
l. responsive to criticism. *
m. recognizes and accepts own limitations. *
n. applies reflection and evaluation to own activities.
o. submits ideas to critical analysis. *

p. describes behavior without inpugning motives.
q. gives constructive criticism without being threatening.
r. makes certain participants want and need evaluation
    before offering it.
s. looks beyond immediate cause and effect relationships.*
t. anticipates problems.
u. enumerates alternative strategies for accomplishing a goal.
v. helps learners evaluate innovations.
w. knows how to question the reality in which we live*
    (employs questioning skills)
x. promotes critical thinking.*
y. stimulates people to decide what they themselves can do
    to satisfy their own wants.
z. develops critical awareness of persons' identity and situation.
aa. develops capacity to analyze causes and consequences of
    one's own situation.
bb. helps participants set goals and reach goals they set.
cc. helps learners perceive opportunities.
dd. tells how to separate useful from non-useful information.
ee. is an analyst of the total situation.
ff. exposes how the oppressed identify with the aspirations
    and values of the oppressor.
gg. involves the people themselves in getting facts they need
    to evaluate a proposed project and decide.
hh. encourages reconsideration of existing plans in the light
    of new information.
ii. is flexible and adaptable.

5. Ability to motivate*

    a. shows enthusiasm and conviction.
    b. mixes entertainment and fun with learning.
    c. enables friendships to be established and maintained.
    d. involves the total personality of the learner in the learning
        process.
    e. inspires others.*
    f. serves as an example of desirable behavior.
    g. relates learning activities to individuals' needs and
        interests.
    h. responds to needs of the participants.
    i. utilizes the experience of the participants.
    j. builds on problems perceived as real.

   k. combines learning and work so that motivation comes from the learning situation.
   l. changes approach when learners appear to be bored.
   m. reinforces participants' behavior.
   n. gives encouragement and guidance but places full responsibility for actual work on participants.
   o. does not try to sell a pre-fixed scheme to people.
   p. maintains high levels of expectations for learners and himself.

6. Group dynamics skills*
   a. establishes an atmosphere of confidence and trust.*
   b. encourages self-respect among participants.*
   c. communicates some sense of openness and accessibility to students.
   d. helps create a sense of group belonging.
   e. encourages openness and exploration.
   f. reduces risk in the group.
   g. discloses personal facts and feelings.
   h. does not condemn.
   i. is responsible to both vocal and quiet members of the group.
   j. emphasizes positive successes of group.
   k. helps the group deal with its own inner conflicts.*
   l. puts tense situation in wider context to relieve tension.
   m. encourages group to talk out anger and despair honestly and openly.
   n. helps conciliate differences in points of view.
   o. helps find compromise solutions.
   p. behaves maturally toward critics in the group.
   q. is not hostile, cynical, or sarcastic.
   r. reduces competitive behavior.
   s. absorbs or drains off feelings of threat.
   t. remains alert to expressions indicative of strong feelings.
   u. relates in an honest and genuine way.*
   v. shares thoughts and feelings simply and in ways which participants may take or leave.
   w. contributes to the personal feelings of security in others.
   x. adjusts the interchange to the tolerance levels of the reactors.
   y. accepts and integrates all expression whether intellectual or emotional.
   z. helps to elicit and clarify the purposes of participants and the group.

aa. encourages participation by all.

bb. maintains a lively group.*

cc. builds cohesiveness of group by improving quality
of interactions among the members.

dd. improves interpersonal relationships.

ee. helps group members learn to communicate with each
other and to work harmoniously and effectively.

ff. helps people become sensitive to group processes.

gg. helps the group to define its own limitations.

hh. goes along with group decision.

ii. summarizes what group feeling is sensed to be.

jj. helps make decisions effectively.

kk. expresses standards for the group to use in choosing its
content or procedures or in evaluating its decisions.

ll. helps meaure group decisions against group standards.

mm. balances own time among the pursuit of goals, the structure
of the organization, and the needs of its members.

nn. evolves from group leader to group participant.

oo. enables leadership to develop within the group.

pp. increases confidence in one's ability to deal with change.

qq. aware of nonfunctional behavior in groups: hostility;
criticizing or blaming others in order to gain status;
deflating the ego of others; citing personal experiences
unrelated to the problem; arguing too much on a point;
rejecting ideas without consideration; competing with
others to talk most, play the most roles; gain favor with
the leader; seeking sympathy, disparaging one's ideas
to gain support; lobbying; using group for one's own pet
concerns or philosophies; clowning; mimicking, joking to
gain attention; loud or excessive talking; extreme ideas;
unusual behavior in order to call attention to oneself;
acting indifferent or passive; daydreaming; whispering
to others; wandering from the subject.

rr. ability to detect phoniness and dishonesty.

ss. does not dominate.*

tt. does not impose a solution.

uu. does not direct meetings.

vv. knows when to serve as an indirect leader rather than as
the visible leader.

ww. knows when not to intervene.

xx. does not accept an office in any group (deprives other
members of the group of a valuable learning opportunity).

yy. stimulates activity but remains in the background.
zz. stresses the importance and the centrality of the
learner and his experience.
aaa. involves people in decisions. *
bbb. enables learning that is self-initiated and self-directed
by the learner.

7. Able to effect horizontal relationships. *
   a. is able to participate and share on the same basis
   as others. *
   b. is not defensive. *
   c. does not put others down.
   d. clearly and consistently demonstrates a real desire to
   help others.
   e. admits he has no answers.
   f. tries at all times to remain acceptable to all members.
   g. views self as a learner.
   h. is able to learn from the learners and all other people.
   i. prizes the learner, his feelings, his person.
   j. accepts and trusts participants.
   k. is able to empathize with participants.
   l. disposes of the dichotomy between student and teacher,
   does not lecture nor make curricular decisions. *
   m. cares for others in a non-possessive way.
   n. shares power and prestige; is a friend. *
   o. encourages others to use power constructively.
   p. encourages others to do act as facilitators. *
   q. shares life situation and personal background. *
   r. lives the lifestyle of the community. *
   s. informal in relations with others.
   t. does not use the community for personal gain. *
   nor use own position to exploit. *
   u. does not show favoritism to any participants.
   v. involves others in planning, decision-making and
   evaluation of their actions. *
   w. never does board work which can be done by student.
   x. speaks in a voice as low as the learner.
   y. does not tell a learner what the learner already knows.
   z. never asks a question twice.
   aa. is friendly, warm, responsive, praising, agreeable,
   accepting. .
   bb. willing to avoid prominence or start with it then retire
   as other people grow in initiative and confidence. *
   cc. does not keep secrets from others.

dd. increases amount of participant planning.
ee. goes along with group decisions.
ff. gives credit to others and to the group.
gg. is pleasant, gregarious, does not preach, is natural. *
hh. is accountable to peers. *
ii. explores a variety of viewpoints.
jj. is patient, unassuming and humble.
kk. gives others the opportunity to serve as co-facilitators in leading groups.
ll. always in close contact with others. *
mm. recognizes that the helping situation is a joint exploration.
nn. reduces competitive behavior.
oo. identifies and opposes paternalism and dependence.
pp. combats social, economic and political domination.
qq. opposes authoritarianism, privilege, and elitist forms of leadership.
rr. helps people to act together for a voice in the decisions affecting their lives.
ss. helps people to reject their roles as oppressed.
tt. reveals the vulnerability and humaness of the oppressor.
uu. reflects values conflicting with the status quo and elites.

8. Problem-solving activity skills.
    a. helps identify problem.
    b. uses force-field diagnostic technique.
    c. helps generate possible alternatives.
    d. employs brainstorm technique.
    e. develops desire and ability to take advantage of existing resources without waiting for everything to come from above.
    f. relates own experiences to group problem.
    g. considers consequences of each solution.
    h. encourages people to accept responsibility to attack problem.
    i. helps choose most likely solution.
    j. seeks a compromise solution.
    k. encourages participants to develop general large scale goals as well as specific limited goals.
    l. helps plan action.
    m. helps determine appropriate steps.
    n. strengthens incentives for people to act.
    o. encourages decision-making behavior of participants.
    p. encourages personal action.
    q. aids in organizing to attack the problem.

    r. helps carry out plan.
    s. encourages the trying of various approaches.
    t. is not easily discouraged. *
    u. able to overcome critical situations. *
    v. supports self-discipline.
    w. helps people deal with social institutions.
    x. acts logically and reflectively to transform reality.
    y. encourages group to follow through to solve problem.
    z. stimulates a process of self-determination and self-help.
  aa. stands up for his rights.
  bb. evaluates outcomes.
  cc. sees knowledge as a process, not an object to possess.

9. Skill in dealing with diverse individual needs and abilities. *
    a. makes an effort to discover the true interests, motivations and wishes of participants.
    b. elicits and clarifies learners' purposes for learning.
    c. helps people identify own growth needs and goals.
    d. plans activities to work towards individuals' goals.
    e. gives encouragement and guidance but places full responsibility for actual work on participants.
    f. sympathizes with learners on both emotional and intellectual levels.
    g. provides support, responsible freedom.
    h. develops committment and self-insight.
    i. insures that the learner will experience success.
    j. respects other people. *
    k. accepts idiosyncratic behavior.
    l. honors the individuality of each person.
    m. helps make people aware of their own self-directing capabilities.
    n. gives greatest consideration to interests and concerns of the learner.
    o. has patience with own frustrations. *
    p. helps people to become inquirers.
    q. prefers a participative life style. *
    r. acts as a guide and coach.
    s. recognizes achievements of participants.
    t. recognizes student strengths.
    u. not threatened by more experienced or knowledgeable people. *
    v. not preoccupied with own needs. *
    w. creative. *

    x. helps arbitrate conflicting individual needs.

    y. does not neglect slower, less-involved learners.

    z. helps people to become conscious of their rights and responsibilities as citizens of a free country.

  aa. relates learning to daily life.

  bb. helps others learn literacy & numeracy skills.

  cc. helps people prepare for and secure better jobs.

10. Able to increase peoples' self-confidence.*

    a. accepts and respects each person.

    b. supports thecontributions of participants.

    c. gives positive reinforcement to participants.

    d. is non-authoritarian.*

    e. communicates confidence in others.*

    f. is friendly, warm, responsive, praising, agreeable, accepting.

    g. speaks in a voice as low as the learner.

    h. is not hostile, cynical or sarcastic.

    i. is willing to find personal satisfaction in the achievements of others even though this may mean lack of credit to himself.

    j. never makes fun of another person or idea.

    k. encourages participants to take more active roles.*

    l. creates independence rather than dependence in participants.

    m. gives learners the opportunity to develop values, attitudes, and standards of behavior on their own.

    n. helps the learner take responsibility for own education and make the necessary decisions.

    o. gives feedback about strengths.

    p. allows learner to carry on the behavior to be learned.

    q. increases the amount of planning done by learners.

    r. makes sure learners have responsible freedom and the opportunity for exploration and success.

    s. helps develop commitment and self-insight.

    t. not threatening to personal behavioral innovations.

    u. inspires confidence.*

    v. bolsters confidence by testing learner on what the learner already knows.

    w. recognizes creativity.

    x. never asks a question twice.

    y. helps each person to accept and respect own self.

    z. assists people in developing favorable self-images.

  aa. emphasizes self awareness and power to control environment.

  bb. encourages union among participants.

  cc. reveals the vulnerability and humanness of the oppressor.

dd. helps people reject that they are "things" owned by the oppressor.

ff. rejects opinions which the oppressor holds of the oppressed.

gg. overcomes own fears and superstitions.

B. Enabling a Learning Environment (Facilitators' Indirect Intervention or Preparation for Learning Group)

11. Able to catalyze cooperation among participants.*
   a. helps individuals work with others effectively and harmoniously.
   b. overcomes individualism when it works against the community.*
   c. encourages people to work together for the common good.
   d. aids in cooperative activity.
   e. does not make assignments.
   f. encourages organization among participants.

12. Materials development skills.
   a. provides a variety of useful materials and activities.
   b. uses materials and methods appropriate to NFE.
   c. provides for choices (options) for learning.
   d. provides challenging materials that are not too difficult.
   e. makes materials and activities enjoyable.
   f. mixes entertainment and fun with learning.
   g. makes use of conventional and unconventional resources.
   h. recognizes the educational utility of the surrounding environment.
   i. uses materials based on local reality, interests, and concerns.
   j. uses materials which are flexible and adaptable to changing circumstances.
   k. relies on learner feedback to determine content, types of materials, and kinds of learning settings which are most appropriate.
   l. allows content to be tested by participants on a trial basis before complete commitment is made.
   m. chooses materials so that cost to participants is low, benefits are high, benefits are immediate, content is simple.
   n. adapts and revises materials so that interest is maintained over a relatively long time period.
   o. provides materials which are self-explanatory.
   p. provides a chance to experience the connecting links between various actions and the outcomes which follow.

q. provides a place where village conflicts can be discussed without confronting individuals directly.

r. provides a setting in which new and unfamiliar actions can be tried without risk.

s. uses materials and activities whereby new learners can be easily integrated, but at the same time more advanced learners can be challenged.

t. is divergent and creative.*

u. uses materials as means rather than as ends.

v. concerned with job mobility.

w. is task or skill centered rather than academically and abstractly oriented.

x. helps learners generate and adapt materials.

13. Able to broaden access to information.

a. is aware of tools available and waysof using them.*

b. secures and distributes literature.

c. encourages active searching.

d. tells how to obtain information for use in decisions and actions.

e. promotes reading newspapers & magazines and listening to the radio.

f. develops a reference service to educational objects available.

g. facilitates communication among people.*

h. helps people realize that they can learn from people and materials already available locally.

i. serves as a "guide" or "coach" rather than drill-master or substitute for a textbook.

j. regards self as a flexible resource to be used by the group.

k. available to help learners with individual problems.

l. provides a forum where issues of concern are discussed.

m. forms small secondary groups around tasks or interests.

n. forms groups for neglected people (young children, out-of-schoolers, girls).

o. forms clubs.

p. organizes school equivalency programs.

q. organizes literacy classes.

r. provides motivating environment.

s. stimulates learners to learn new ways of learning.

t. helps individuals take responsibility for own growth.

u. brings individuals to awareness of self-directing capabilities.

v. stress choice, initiative, and freedom to explore.

w. promotes learning by doing, self initiated learning, and student self-evaluation.

x. helps participants learn how to learn.

261

y. helps learner achieve independence.
z. sees knowledge as a process, not an object to possess.
aa. helps parents to become educators in their families.
bb. helps participants learn skills of "studenting":

1. ability to concentrate during class sessions to learn materials
2. ability to discriminate between relative importance of materials
3. ability to sum up key points in an understandable fashion
4. knowledge of what study resources are available and where to find them
5. ability to use study facilities to maximum effect
6. knowledge of alternative learning options and ability to use them as aids to learning
7. ability to relate facts and experiences to strategies already internalized, in order to solve problems
8. ability to generate new and unique uses of materials
9. ability to evaluate materials with awareness of religious, cultural, political, philosophical, etc., bias
10. ability to clearly state one's knowledge orally
11. ability to make stimulating comments in discussion sessions
12. ability to ask what one desires to learn
13. ability to ask challenging questions concerning weakness in the argument
14. ability to effectively explain material to another individual
15. excitement about learning and discovering for oneself
16. viewing materials as others see them
17. forming positive learning relationships with other students learners
18. ability to determine study objectives and complete them
19. the ability of the student to believe in his competence and skill to study well.
20. knowing one's own personal learning objectives
21. ability to be clear minded and consistent in expressing one's overall attitudes and priorities
22. ability to follow through personal priorities conscientiously
23. ability to grant equal tolerance and respect to the views of other students
24. having a positive sense of working with teachers and peers as a team in the pursuit of learning.

cc. promotes learning in different situations.
dd. varies the meeting room according to purpose.
ee. makes physical environment more pleasant.
ff. organizes learning opportunities on site close to implementation.

14. Skill in a variety of learning techniques.*
   a. provides options for individual learners.*
   b. has a flexible attitude towards the organization of educational experiences.
   c. provides for individual study.*
   d. provides opportunities for students teaching students.
   e. spends more time on providing learning resources than preparing lesson plans.
   f. organizes learning opportunities on site close to implementation.
   g. is creative.*
   h. prefers learning by doing.
   i. is familiar with the six-step modified Ashton-Warner literacy method.
   j. employs specific techniques and media*: apprenticeship, audience reaction teams, brainstorming, buzz sessions, bulletin boards, bush academy, learning contracts, ceremonies, case studies, circular letter or other direct mail, correspondence courses, colloquies, committees, conferences, conventions, campaigns, demonstrations (result and method), daycare center, discussion groups, directed individual studies, chalkboard, ethnic theater, field trips or tours, forums, exhibits, film-strips, flip charts, flannelboard, film, field days, farm visits, group study, guerrilla theater, institutes, interviews, individual conferences, home visits, lectures or speeches, listening teams, library service, learning module, judging contests, magazines, newspapers, mobile units, music, on-the-job visits, panels, plays, puppets, posters, publications, programmed instruction, quizzes, photography and drawing, personal letter, recording devices, radio, role plays, question periods, short courses, slides, seminars, skits, symposia, teachins, television, simulations, skill exchange, technological center in the village, and workshops.

15. Skill in pacing (regulating movement from one part of a learning experience to the next).
   a. determines pace through observation of the learners.

b. allows participants time to digest information and suggestions.
c. lets student set his own pace.
d. does not allow group to flounder.

C. Relating to the Community (outside the learning group).

16. Able to discover and articulate the learning needs present in the community. (employs analytical and evaluation skills)
   a. observes and records contradictions present in the community.
   b. identifies changing local needs.
   c. acquaints villagers with their problems.
   d. helps establish learning goals and objectives.

17. Skill in building community support. *
   a. establishes rapport with the community. *
   b. gives reasons for own concerns and community work. *
   c. is accountable to the community. *
   d. provides the community with information concerning own activities.
   e. tests ideas before launching projects.
   f. patient in dealing with factions.
   g. curbs natural eagerness to get things moving quickly.
   h. sponsors some activities which will show quick results.
   i. can absorb defeats without losing commitment. *
   j. keeps aloof from internal politics of the village.
   k. remains neutral in factional quarrels.
   l. able to get NFE ideas accepted.
   m. is accountable to peers. *
   n. respected by peers because he respects them. *
   o. is reliable, consistent, and honest. *
   p. relates to individuals at all levels of society.
   q. does not bully people into participating. *
   r. has a presence as a person which tends to counter apathy and fear. *
   s. assists and enables the powerless.
   t. does not threaten authorities. *
   u. overcomes opposition of authorities. *

18. Skill in working with community leaders. *
   a. works with all factions. *
   b. organizes an advisory committee of keen and influential local people.
   c. includes assisting cooperators in the planning stage.
   d. gives full credit to those who help.
   e. seeks guidance.

f. safeguards the status of the community's traditional leaders.
g. gives as much attention to leaders who do not sympathize with his aims as those who do.
h. does not favor any one leader at the expense of any rival leaders.
i. seeks direct or indirect participation of established community leaders in all activities.
j. does not neglect any interest group or constituency.

19. Able to stimulate family planning related to solving family problems.
    a. imparts information relevant to family needs:*
        1. child care, sanitation, nutrition,
        2. family planning,
        3. protecting family health,
        4. care of the injured and sick,
        5. intelligent shopping and use of money,
        6. making clothes and other consumption goods,
        7. house repairs and environmental improvements,
        8. growing and preserving food for family consumption,
        9. knowledge of the concept of unit price.
    b. suggests home projects.
    c. organizes literacy classes.
    d. urges adoption of proven ideas.
    e. facilitates numeracy required for market settings.
    f. helps individuals increase their standard of living.
    g. discourages conspicuous consumption.
    h. encourages thrift and savings.
    i. helps people increase their material well-being and productivity.
    j. helps people prepare for and secure better jobs.
    k. works with village women and village families.
    l. ensures that members base thinking on facts not assumptions.

20. Able to stimulate community organization.
    a. works through the local culture (values those aspects which are important locally)
    b. encourages community loyalty and solidarity.
    c. emphasizes the common interest.
    d. encourages communal decisions and communal actions.
    e. goes along with group decisions.
    f. helps community define the type of leadership needed for specific jobs and stimulates people to recruit those leaders.
    g. encourages local capacity and self reliance.
    h. supports local control of and responsibility for education.
    i. encourages greater shared leadership.

      j. obtains more active participation by women.
      k. provides information about civic participation.
      l. shows how to keep records.
      m. is an instigator of processes.

21. Skill in aiding community planning.*
      a. works within the cultural and historical traditions of a society.
      b. looks for solutions from within the community.
      c. perceptive of social forces in the community.*
      d. tries to discover and push community needs rather than personal ones.
      e. helps find a solution acceptable to the community.
      f. helps the community to make use of its resources.
      g. encourages active participation and joint planning.
      h. encourages dialogue among community members.*
      i. creates activities involving community reflection on its needs and concerns.*
      j. provides emotional, physical, and philosophical support in assessing needs and concerns.*
      k. facilitates community decisions with a broad base of input.*
      l. provides a forum where issues of concern are discussed.
      m. submits anticipated project to thorough group discussion.
      n. encourages openness and exploration and objectivity.
      o. seeks clarification of values, ideas, and information.
      p. expresses standards for the community to use.
      q. tries to draw together activities of various subgroups or members.
      r. ensures that members base thinking on facts not assumptions.
      s. assesses practicality of project in terms of local situation, skills, resources, and anticipated difficulties.
      t. considers what skills people will need in order to adopt the innovation successfully (how many people will need them, who is competent and available to teach them, how best they can be learned).
      u. considers whether the project will benefit only some of the people.
      v. occasionally advocates solutions responsive to local conditions when needed.
      w. suggests new ideas and new definitions of the problem and new attacks on the problem.
      x. imparts information relevant to community needs.*
      y. tries to envision how an idea might work.
      z. stimulates people to think and act positively.*

22. Able to catalyze community projects. *
    a. relates own experience to group problem.
    b. suggests community projects.
    c. innovates solutions more responsive to local conditions.
    d. promotes projects desired by the whole community.
    e. becomes involved in community action programs or activities. *
    f. sweats with the community. *
    g. understands how things get done in the village and society. *
    h. can absorb defeats and problems without losing commitments. *
    i. patient with own frustrations. *
    j. maintains enthusiasm for a project over time.
    k. stimulates the community to take responsibility for its own affairs.
    l. plays the role of a social agitator.
    m. provides information about civic participation.
    n. organizes cooperatives.
    o. stimulates people to think and act positively. *
    p. wins the confidence of people holding opposite views in the village.
    q. strives to meet community goals. *
    r. makes suggestions as to what others might do for the community.

D. Organization and Administration (which support all other activities)

   23. Able to bring people together. *
       a. recruits participants.
       b. skilled in arranging for locale (building, site, etc.) for sessions.
       c. provides for opportune scheduling.
       d. organizes and holds learning sessions.
       e. encourages people to drop in on learning activites.
       f. provides flexibility in timing of activities.
       g. structures sessions at times conducive to wide participation.
       h. meets individual and group needs.
       i. enables friendships to be established and maintained.
       j. maintains a lively group. *
       k. coordinates group activities with community's activities.
       l. supplements or complements formal schooling.
       m. works closely with formal educational programs.
       n. organizes school equivalency programs.

24. Able to simultaneously pursue multiple goals.
    a. well organized but not rigid.
    b. does not overload self.
    c. is realistic in deciding what to do.
    d. seeks the help of specialists.
    e. delegates responsibility.
    f. able to work in relatively unstructured situations or
       provide own structure.
    g. flexibility and activities.
    h. does not need structure.*
    i. balances time between the pursuit of goals and the structure
       of the organization and the needs of its members.
    j. does not get bogged down in infighting and organizational
       concerns.

25. Ability to match learning needs to learning resources and
    opportunities.*
    a. understands how to use resources.*
    b. uses materials opportunely.*
    c. checks compatability of resources with clients' needs.
    d. acts as a broker--puts people in touch with resources.
    e. makes use of conventional and unconventional resources.
    f. develops a reference service to educational objects and
       educators which are available.

26. Skill in planning NFE activities
    a. understands how to work with committees.
    b. ensures that members base thinking on facts not assumptions.
    c. encourages objectivity.
    d. develops a plan for each year's activities.
    e. sets realistic goals.*
    f. is clear about objectives which are clearly defined.
    g. explores alternatives.
    h. understands personal goals, participants' goals, and
       program goals.*
    i. can predict obstacles and successes.
    j. investigates difficulties which caused previous failures.
    k. stresses need to find and investigate every possible snag
       in order to ensure that the project should succeed.
    l. attends to practical details.
    m. able to look at a problem and detach it from family ties and
       values.
    n. able to draw out the right conclusions.

    o. is an analyst of the total situation.
    p. considers the timing of projects.
    q. delays introduction until there is a good chance of success.
    r. evaluates program and performance on continuous basis.
    s. able to diagnose the cause of failures.
    t. aware of alternative overall organization of efforts.

27. Able to develop a communication network. *
    a. participates in a support group with other facilitators regularly at a fixed time.
    b. maintains contact with others doing the same work. *
    c. seeks followup, supervision, and advice for self-improvement.
    d. develops own nonformal communication network to provide new ideas and information or plug into existing system.
    e. seeks the help of specialists.
    f. asks for help only when needed.
    g. has contacts with institutions working in development.
    h. encourages communication with other villages for ideas and support.
    i. includes assisting cooperators in planning stage.
    j. gives full credit to cooperators who help.
    k. utilizes external agencies. *
    l. able to work with local and national voluntary organizations.
    m. obtains information from radio and newspapers.
    n. organizes women's groups.
    o. works with learners from all age groups.
    p. forms groups for neglected groups (young children, out-of-schoolers, girls).
    q. initiates reflection groups.

28. Functional literacy and numeracy skills.
    a. can keep records of receipts and disbursements.
    b. has accounting skills.
    c. strives to make the program self-sufficient economically.
    d. helps the community to become self-sufficient economically.
    e. can keep written notes on activities.

29. Negotiation skills. *
    a. is able to get a reasonable hearing from organizational representatives, politicians, educators, social services.
    b. is frank and serene in dealing with authorities and superiors. *
    c. does not lose temper.
    d. has own position well thought out in advance.
    e. states position clearly and firmly.

f. knows what adversary will agree to.
g. persistent--doesn't accept all excuses and regulations.
h. able to detect phoniness and dishonesty.
i. checks for hidden assumptions and biases.
j. looks for incongruities.

30. Training skills
   a. develops commited local leaders.
   b. trains group leaders.
   c. trains in committee procedures.
   d. assigns leadership responsibilities.
   e. provides the right roles to stimulate the emergence of more leadership.
   f. enables leadership to develop within the group.
   g. forms small groups around tasks or interests.
   h. identifies and trains youth leaders.
   i. trains youth for leadership.
   j. trains facilitators for other villages.
   k. can organize training programs for new facilitators: locate facilities, hire cook, buy food, plan the course, and prepare and negotiate the budget).
   l. helps learners become trainers and facilitators for other learners.
   m. trains in record keeping.
   n. knows about group organization and leadership development.
   o. helps people learn how to give help.

E. Knowledge

31. Knows NFE from formal education.
   a. has a style of presentation that is in contrast to the "teacher."*
   b. is a friend in place of a teacher.*
   c. does not set lesson tasks, assign readings, lecture or expound unless requested to, evaluate and criticize unless a student wishes it, take full responsibility for exams, or grades, etc.
   d. emphasizes the differences in own role from that of a traditional teacher.
   e. centers learning on content rather than on the teacher.
   f. stresses acculturation as opposed to enculturation.
   g. stresses resocialization as opposed to socialization.
   h. believes in decision making at the local level. *
   i. knows the advantages and disadvantages between formal and nonformal education.
   j. has critically assimilated the objectives of facilitator training.

32. Aware of what other individuals, groups, and communities have done to improve themselves.
    a. knows of outside agencies, groups, and individuals of potential service.
    b. aware of useful changes in neighboring communities.
    c. knows of group organization and leadership development alternatives.

33. Possesses knowledge of areas pertinent to development.
    a. farm planning and management.
    b. use of credit; application of new technology; storage; processing; food preservation; government policies, programs and services; family improvement (health, nutrition, home economics, family planning, child care); cooperatives; and local and national government operation.

F. Attitudes

34. Sensitive to the feelings, attitudes, and relationships of people.
    a. can see the learning potential in individuals of diverse backgrounds and life styles.
    b. respects each person's individuality.
    c. sees people as subjects not objects; as ends, not means.
    d. is responsible to both vocal and quiet members of the group.
    e. patient, non-partisan, devoted to people, on the side of the good that can be shared by everyone.
    f. constantly seeks to increase own sensitivity.
    g. understands human nature.*
    h. understands human relations and group dynamics.
    i. knows that disunion works against the individual.
    j. sees leadership as performance of acts which help the group achieve its preferred outcomes.
    k. sees leadership as an event rather than a style or person.
    l. able to defend the learning group from excessive or obtrusive intervention by outside evaluators and foreign visitors.
    m. rejects opinions which the oppressor holds of the oppressed.
    n. helps the people achieve independence from the oppressor.
    o. believes that dehumanization can be prevented.
    p. helps people reject aggression against their own kind.
    q. able to empathize--see other person's point of view.
    r. concerned with group and community needs.*

35. Believes people should constantly aspire to improve themselves and their environment.
    a. believes in change.*
    b. aware of the sequence for change agent roles:
        1. develops need for change,
        2. establishes a change relationship,
        3. diagnoses the problem,
        4. creates in the learner the intent to change,
        5. translates intent into action,
        6. stabilizes change and prevents discontinuances,
        7. achieves a terminal relationship.
    c. plans for change.
    d. shares information relating to the need for change.
    e. has faith in the probability that other people will become better if encouraged with sufficient skill.
    f. believes certain processes help people better themselves.
    g. hopes people will exercise more control over change rather than be victims of it.
    h. helps people perceive their state not as fated and unalterable, but merely as limiting and therefore challenging.
    i. emphasizes self-awareness and power to control.
    j. helps people to see that they are responsible for the world and can transform the world.
    k. helps people increase their material well-being and productivity.
    l. combines reflection with action.
    m. fosters a scientific outlook.
    n. knows that freedom is a sequential relationship between perceiving and acting.
    o. encourages participants to try proven ideas.
    p. emphasizes wise use of natural resources.
    q. appreciates and upholds the dignity of physical labor and other necessary activities of production.
    r. stress the importance and centrality of the learner and his experience.
    s. encourages desire for education and self-education as values.
    t. stimulates learners' aspirations.
    u. increases the number of functional literates.
    v. provides for inculcation of moral values.
    w. reflects values conflicting with the status quo and elites.
    x. overcomes own fears and supersititions.*

36. Actively seeks out sources of information, material, or resistance
    critical to individual or community development.
    a. utilizes external agencies.*
    b. seeks out assistance of institutions for community development.
    c. skilled in dealing with institutions.*
    d. willing to approach the appropriate source of information.
    e. seeks out necessary information but does not use it as a
       powerholding technique.*
    f. is not afraid of officials or powerful men.
    g. knows how to get petitions written and delivered to the
       appropriate authorites.
    h. maintains a healthy scepticism (critical analysis) to recommenda-
       tions from outside experts.
    i. keeps external threats to learning at a minimum.
    j. strong in standing up to authorities.*
    k. is frank and serene in dealing with authorities and superiors.*
    l. is not submissive to authorities.*
    m. impertinent, but knows productive limits of insouciance.*
    n. advocates human rights.*
    o. stands up for own rights.
    p. strong in standing up against members of higher social classes.*
    q. advocates the culture of the community.*
    r. tells how to use to their advantage the existing political and
       legal system.
    s. acts as an advocate especially to help someone who is in the
       minority and disenfranchised.
    t. confronts pessimism and fatalism.
    u. knows what an oppressed person is like and looks for
       liberating action.

37. Sees development as a process of liberation from domination and
    dependence.
    a. knows that education is not and cannot be neutral.
    b. sees schools as instruments of social control.
    c. believes education should liberate, not domesticate.
    d. understands the role of institutions (especially church and
       school) in maintaining the existing system.*
    e. rejects oppression.*
    f. aims at social justice, self-reliance, more equitable
       distribution of wealth, and participation of people in decisions
       which affect their lives.
    g. exposes how the oppressed identify with the aspirations and
       values of the oppressor.
    h. knows that oppression is not simply the situation itself,
       it is also the perception of the situation by the oppressed.

i. sees development as something people do for themselves with or without outside help.
j. encourages the participation of the poorest people in the community.
k. advocates community development. *
l. encourages rural youth to invest themselves in rural areas rather than transfering to the city.
m. sees own rewards as tied directly to the community's development. *

APPENDIX B

OPERATIONALIZATION WORKBOOK

APPENDIX B

SELF-INSTRUCTIONAL MODULE FOR LEARNING THE HUTCHINSON
METHOD OF OPERATIONALIZING A GOAL OR INTENT

Richard T. Coffing, Thomas E. Hutchinson, James B. Thomann
and Richard G. Allan

Produced under the Direction of Richard T. Coffing and
James M. Cooper

School of Education, University of Massachusetts
June 1971

HOW TO USE THE MODULE

The purpose of this self-instructional module is to help you learn how
to break down a goal into its directly observable component parts. These parts
of the goal can then be used as evaluative criteria for measuring accomplishment
of the goal.

You, the reader, will not want to proceed further unless you believe
your purposes coincide with the purpose of the module. As a guideline on
whether to continue, you might ask yourself right now, "Do I, or does any
decision-maker I work with, have a goal or an intention that I want to see
accomplished by the program I am working on?" If your answer to that question
is "No", then the module clearly is not for you.

If your answer is "Yes," then ask yourself the question, "If I were to
tell that goal to someone else and ask him to find out whether that goal was
being accomplished, would he come back to me with the same information that
I would bring back if I were checking on the goal?" If your answer to that
question is "Yes," and if you can have the same thing happen for other goals
too, then you probably do not need to study this module. But if the answer to
that second question is "NO," then the module is intended for you.

If you have decided now to study the module, there is still another question which you should ask yourself: "Given a choice, do I prefer to learn by reading and doing, or by listening and doing?" If you prefer to learn by reading and doing, then be sure you have possession of the "Self-contained Workbook (Option A);" you should use that workbook to learn the procedure. However, if you prefer to learn by listening and doing, then make sure you have both the "Audio Cassette for Use with Audio Workbook (Option B)" and the "Audio Workbook (Option B)." All the instructions you have read so far are identical for the two instructional alternatives, so you should check the cover now to be sure you have the materials for the option you prefer.

The procedure which you will experience during this self-instructional module is a new method for operationally defining goals. This is a specific application of a general method developed by Thomas E. Hutchinson, Associate Professor of Education, University of Massachusetts, which he calls "The Operationalization of Fuzzy Concepts," for reasons that will be obvious when you do the procedure.

When you have at least an hour to spend on the module, then continue reading these instructions--in the workbook which you have chosen to use. Whichever workbook you choose, be sure to proceed through it page by page, without pre-viewing, skimming or skipping. Experience has shown that exposure to the material without doing the procedure step by step can lose to the reader many of the benefits of this procedure.

When you are ready to begin, think of a goal or intention that you want to work with. It may be easiest for you to use the one which appears as the example in this module: "helping others." But you may choose your own if you wish; it should be one which has some importance to you and it should be "good and fuzzy," for purposes of learning the procedure. Write it down someplace. (Sometimes when the goal is not written down, it changes in the process of operationalization.) If your goal is not "helping others," then when the term "helping others" appears in the following pages you should substitute mentally the goal which you have written down.

The first step is to construct in your mind a hypothetical situation. This hypothetical situation should be as real and as complete as possible--with people in it, furniture, a complete environment. It might be inside or outside; that doesn't matter. It should not be too specific--a general hypothetical situation. Now, in this hypothetical situation a person is "helping others." In fact, this person is the epitome of "helping others." This person is the best that you can imagine that "helping others" could possibly be. What I want you to do is to examine the hypothetical situation, observe it very carefully, and write down all the things that you see about that person, about that person's interaction with other people, about the environment, about interaction between people and the environment, anything at all going on that would indicate to you that "helping others" is present, that the person really is "helping others." And just write them down on a list. Do this now on the next page.

WRITE DOWN THE THINGS YOU SEE THAT INDICATE TO YOU THAT THE FUZZY CONCEPT IS PRESENT. Be sure to exhaust the hypothetical situation. Don't just put down the first two or three things that come to mind. Get everything out of it that you can.

WHEN YOU HAVE EXHAUSTED THIS PROCESS, PROCEED TO THE NEXT PAGE.

If you were trying to operationalize "helping others" completely, you would not move on to a second step until the first one had been completely exhausted, with everything out of it you could possibly get.

By the first step, you may have identified some of the dimensions you have for "helping others" at this first level of breakdown. As the early steps in

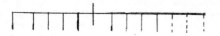

the procedure are completed, you will have found more and more of the dimensions; in later steps you may have more difficulty in finding others. You should not necessarily expect each of the later steps to elicit the same quantity of dimensions that you get at the first stage.

The second step of the procedure is to construct a second hypothetical situation. Again, it should be as complete as possible. There should be people; they should be doing things, interacting with each other; there should be a complete environment. It may be inside or outside. It should have anything you want to put into this environment--except, in this hypothetical situation, there is no "helping others" going on at all. A complete absence of "helping others." What I want you to do is to examine this situation, observe it carefully and write down all the things you can see in this situation that indicate to you that "helping others" is absent. Don't just write down the negative ends of positive dimensions that you thought up in the first situation. Use the second hypothetical situation to identify a wider range of dimensions of "helping others" than you got from the first step. Use the next page to write your list.

WRITE DOWN THE THINGS YOU SEE THAT INDICATE TO YOU THAT THE FUZZY CONCEPT IS ABSENT. Again, try to exhaust the situation; get everything out of it that is available in it.

WHEN YOU HAVE EXHAUSTED THIS PROCESS, PROCEED TO THE NEXT PAGE.

By doing the second step you may have identified some more of the dimensions

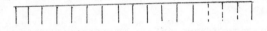

that you have for "helping others." With each succeeding step, there will be fewer left, and they will be harder and harder to find.

Some parts of the procedure will work better for you than others will. Also, for different fuzzy concepts, different aspects of the procedure will work better than others. For example, there are some fuzzy concepts where the negative hypothetical situation gets all the dimensions and the positive gets few; and there are others where the positive situation gets most of the dimensions and the negative gets few. So for that reason I advise against skipping any of the steps. Only when you have had enough experience with it for a large number of instances, is it safe to say that this particular part doesn't work for you. If some part doesn't work for you, then don't do it; but at first give it a good workout because, for example, if the first three times you use in part two doesn't work, that doesn't mean that it won't work when the next fuzzy concept that comes along that you want to deal with. It may very well be the most important step for that one, so give it a good chance before you rule out any one of the steps for your own practice. But if you do get a consistent history of a certain step not doing anything for you, then obviously you should eliminate it.

The third step in the procedure is to get two or three other people to go through steps one and two, the positive and negative hypothetical situations, whereby they operationalize in part what they mean by "helping others"--their dimensions for it. Then you take their lists and look at each item--one by one--and you ask yourself the following question, "Is this an item I want on my list; Is this a dimension that I have, really?" This is just another way of finding additional dimensions.

Of course there are a number of possibilities for each item on another person's list. You may already have it on your list. You may find one that you would really like to have, so you add it to your list. You may find one that is not on your list and you don't want it. In fact, you can't stand it. In fact, it makes you so angry that you think of two or three more of your own dimensions, and of course you add them to your list. The point is that you identify all the dimensions that you have for the fuzzy concept. You are not agreeing or disagreeing with the other people. You are using their lists as stimuli to yourself, so that you can consider each of their dimensions and say, "This is one of mine, but I didn't think of it before." Or you say, "This one is ridiculous--it makes me think of three that I hadn't thought of before," and so you add them. And of course the last possibility is that it's not on your list and you don't want it and it doesn't make you think of a blessed thing. Now review this last paragraph and do the procedure. (If there are no other people from whom you can get lists at this moment, then stop here temporarily until you are able to get them.) Use the next page in the workbook to record the additions to your list. Do not discuss or justify your items. This procedure is designed to help you make your list as complete as possible, not to justify your list to anyone else.

ADDITIONS TO YOUR LIST BASED ON COMPARISON WITH OTHERS:

By that last process, you may have found a few more. It can be quite rich.

One thing that might be mentioned is that it is desirable to pick people who do not think the way that you do--why would you want to look only at your own dimensions? That would not help in terms of identification. So pick people who you think will give you some spread, because then you can better examine what your own spread is.

The purpose of the whole operationalization procedure is definitely not to eliminate fuzzy concepts. For one thing, if we had to communicate always at the dimension level, in order to say "hello" it would take a few volumes, and obviously we cannot manage to do that in everyday life. A fuzzy concept is a remarkable, convenient shorthand, although a lot of information gets lost in the process of creating and using one. It is advisable to be aware of this so that you lose less. It is not one of the purposes of the procedure to cause people always to use words precisely the same way, with the same set of dimensions. The process probably can be used, though, to help people get together.

The fourth step in the procedure is harder. In this step, what I want you to do is to go back to the original hypothetical situations you had before, conjure them up again, as it were, and I want you to look at them again because there were things going on in those hypothetical situations that you did not write down because at the moment you did not think that they were part of what you mean by "helping others." I want you to re-examine all the things that you can find in those original hypothetical situations that you did not put down, and seriously examine the implications of those things <u>not</u> being part of what you mean by "helping others."

Here is an example, but it is out of the context of this particular fuzzy concept. Say, I am trying to operationalize someone's concept "success in a job," and he sees himself getting good money, but he does not write that down. It is not one of his listed dimensions of "success in a job." So I'll say to him, "Imagine that you had no money at all, ever;" and usually at that point he is prepared to say, "Well, by not putting it down I didn't quite mean <u>that</u>. I need enough to exist and to live--up to a certain point. After that, it is not important as a dimension of success in a job." So he puts it down and qualifies it: "Money up to $10,000/year" or whatever level is being thought about.

So in this step in the procedure you re-examine the hypothetical situations; you look at the things that are going on, and especially at the things you did not write down. You seriously examine the implications of those things not being part of what you mean by "helping others." Do this now, and use the next page to add to your list.

REEXAMINATION OF ORIGINAL HYPOTHETICAL SITUATIONS:

WHEN YOU HAVE FINISHED THE REEXAMINATION, CONTINUE TO THE NEXT PAGE.

You might have found a few more dimensions by doing the fourth step, but of course there were fewer to find.

You have already identified a lot of dimensions that you have at this first
level of breakdown.

> Because the fifth and last step is the hardest, what I want you
> to do is, after I say the directions, just do it. Don't cognate
> over what it means to do it, just let it happen.

> Here are the directions: I want you to think up dimensions
> that have nothing to do with "helping others," and then
> seriously examine whether or not they do.

RESULTS OF THE STEP:

WHEN YOU HAVE EXHAUSTED THIS PROCESS, CONTINUE TO NEXT PAGE.

Here is one way the step can work. Let us say, for example, I am a
marriage counselor and a fellow comes who is having domestic problems at
home. I have him operationalize what he means by "good father," and he goes
through a positive hypothetical situation and a negative hypothetical situation
and then sees some other people's lists. (Because I've been doing this for 20
years, I have a lot of them handy.) Then he goes back to the hypothetical
situations and looks again at what is going on and examines whether or not the
things that are going on really have anything to do with "good father." So for
about an hour or more he has been immersed in this fuzzy concept. Then I
ask "All right, what has nothing to do with it?" and he replies, "How much
time I spend at home." People don't think up things that have nothing to do
with their concept when you ask them to. Of course, if you cognated over it
long enough, you would think of the pyramids of Egypt or the dark side of the
moon. But if you just let it happen, what would you get? You would get things
that really are related, as a result of the mind-freeing twist of the question,
"What has nothing to do with it?" It may be something, in the case of
counseling, that is a repressed dimension. It may be, in other cases, things
that might be considered frivolous. The frivolous things come up, and you
can examine them seriously. You see, one of the things that we mean in
Western thought by "ridiculous" is "don't think about it," and my suggestion
is that's dangerous. We have to think about such things. The greater our
tendency is to label something ridiculous, probably the more important it is to
consider it very seriously, because it is within that area that we are not
utilizing our thought, not giving it careful consideration.

By this last step, you may have identified some more dimensions and
all I will ever claim is that at the very best, doing the whole procedure carefully

and exhausting each step, you will get a very good approximation to the number of dimensions that you have, what you mean when you use the term "helping others."

Now the next thing to do is to go back to the first item on the first line and look at it--the very first item on the first list. And ask yourself the following question, "Is this either a directly observable behavior or a directly observable state?" Another way to approach it is to ask, "If I said this dimension to someone else and told them 'Go over in that room and tell me if

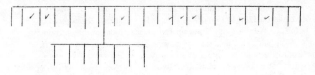

this thing is happening,' would he come back with the same information that I would get if I went myself?" If the answers to these questions are "No," then that item is a fuzzy concept. What you would then do is take that fuzzy concept

and go through the same sequence of five steps to break it down. Usually at the very first level of breakdown for a very fuzzy concept, there will be very few dimensions that are directly observable behaviors or states. However, as you go down the structure, you will gradually get a higher and higher percentage of directly observable behaviors or states until, if you operationalize all of it, you will have a very long, very comprehensive, very complete approximation to the total number of specific behavioral events and states that you mean when you use this term.

Now someone is going to say, "That takes an awful lot of time," or "It's awfully complex." Well, it is YOUR fuzzy concept. If the process is complex, that is because your concept is complex. If your concept is simple, so will this be.

Another possibility is that one may find the original fuzzy concept cropping up again a couple of layers down; nothing ever gets down to observability. Well, that may be because the person has no reality base for the concept that he is using. For instance, if I gave you a fuzzy concept that you had never used, don't use, and that isn't meaningful to you, you would probably be able to go through the process for a while but you would never come down to earth because it is a whurr of verbiage, a whurr of fuzz. It never would touch down to reality because you would have no reality referents that are meaningful to you in terms of that fuzzy concept.

Now go back to the first item on the first list and ask yourself, "Is this a directly observable behavior or state? If I sent someone to find out if this thing were happening, would he come back with the same information that I would get if I went myself." If the answer is "No" to either question, then - you have a fuzzy concept which needs to be broken down further. And so on for the other items on your list. For each item that is still fuzzy, repeat the five-step procedure to get to the second level of breakdown. Do one now, and you can use the next page to begin the procedure.

BEGIN THE PROCEDURE FOR THE SECOND LEVEL OF BREAKDOWN:

If after completing the procedure at the second level of breakdown, you find you still have some dimensions that are not directly observable behaviors or states, then repeat the procedure again with them. At this third level, you may not need to check with other person (Step 3).

You have completed this instructional module. Please follow this advice:

> If you wish to have someone else use this procedure, please do not just describe it to them; have them actually go through the process. A negative reaction can occur when a person only hears the steps described without actually experiencing them.